AESTHETICS

Philosophy

———

Editor

PROFESSOR S. KÖRNER
jur.Dr, Ph.D, FBA
Professor of Philosophy
in the University of Bristol

AESTHETICS

AN INTRODUCTION

W. Charlton

Lecturer in Philosophy
University of Newcastle upon Tyne

HUTCHINSON UNIVERSITY LIBRARY
LONDON

HUTCHINSON & CO (*Publishers*) LTD
178–202 Great Portland Street, London W1

London Melbourne Sydney
Auckland Johannesburg Cape Town
and agencies throughout the world

First published 1970

The picture The Mysterious Vase *on the cover of
the paperback edition is anonymous late nineteenth
century and is reproduced by courtesy of Dr Christa
Pieske*

*This book has been set in Times type, printed in Great Britain
on smooth wove paper by W. Heffer & Sons of Cambridge,
and bound by Wm. Brendon of Tiptree, Essex*
ISBN 0 09 103860 8(cased)
ISBN 0 09 103861 X(paper)

CONTENTS

Contents cont.

PREFACE

Professional philosophers, those, I mean, who practise philosophy rather as an academic discipline than as a way of life, seldom deal with everything which the layman considers to be their concern. Now of one topic, now of another, the complaint is heard: 'Why do philosophers say nothing about this?' Twenty years ago British philosophers were very reluctant to speak of art and beauty. Partly, perhaps, they were deterred by the many and lengthy German writings on aesthetics which have piled up since the eighteenth century and which whether we find them heady or indigestible, are (with a few distinguished exceptions) of limited philosophical interest; partly too by the idea that when you have subtracted all that the art historian and the student of literature may say, nothing remains in aesthetics but personal taste and subjective feeling, matters for treatment, perhaps, in a literary essay, but not in a work of philosophy. At any rate, an excursion into aesthetics was felt to be a form of intellectual slumming.

Today the case has changed. The increase in undergraduates taking philosophy by itself or in conjunction with English, fine art and the like, has created a demand; and the demand has been met by a swelling supply of articles, and more recently monographs, aesthetic in scope but as rigorous as you could wish in method and character. Formerly those teaching aesthetics—I speak for myself, at least—found it hard to know where to begin or end. The field of aesthetics was covered by a thick mist—if it was not what Peacock called a transcendental darkness—through which one groped praying that the problems one's arms closed on might be such as a dialectical training fits one to control. Now definite outlines of a landscape are becoming clear; and it no longer seems wholly rash to offer an introductory book which, like the present one, aspires not only to present, in a form which will allow the modern reader to get his teeth into them, some of the chief ideas put forward by philosophers of the past, but also to indicate a set of prominent problems which are at present receiving or awaiting philosophical attention. Mapping a field of philosophy is, of course, itself a philosophical enterprise, and controversial; but the field must be trodden by a number of explorers who are steady on their feet before the controversy can get under way. That, I am glad to say, seems to be the situation with aesthetics now.

This book is based on lectures given at Trinity College, Dublin, and at the University of Newcastle upon Tyne during the last five years. I am much indebted for their encouragement and comments to those who attended these lectures. Drafts of some sections of the book were read to colleagues in Ireland, and I am grateful for their criticisms. I am also grateful to Dr P. Zinovieff for advice over the sections concerned with music; the views expressed in these sections, however, and such mistakes as lurk in them, are entirely my responsibility.

I

PHILOSOPHICAL AESTHETICS

1. The subject-matter of aesthetics

What is aesthetics about? It is natural for anyone embarking on a study to want to know his terms of reference, but we should not insist on having them made precise at the outset, when that will prejudice the results of our enquiries. Sometimes there is no risk of this. We may say that ornithology is about birds, and we have not prejudged any issues on which ornithologists divide. What ornithology is about is not an ornithological question. But what aesthetics is about seems to be a question belonging to the subject matter of aesthetic discussion. Different aestheticians would wish to return different answers to it, and if we adopt one prematurely, we may find the line we are to take on other aesthetic issues already marked out.

There is such a subject as aesthetics because people sometimes assess and enjoy things aesthetically; and we shall avoid begging any questions if we say that aesthetics is the study of the things we assess aesthetically, and of the grounds and character of aesthetic judgement. It may then, of course, be asked: what do we mean by aesthetic assessment or enjoyment? But we can still keep our pristine freedom of manoeuvre if we reply, not with a formal definition, but with examples. Consider the following cases. You are thinking of taking a flat: you look it over, and note, among other things, that the rooms and windows are well or ill proportioned. You are driving somewhere on business, and see that the countryside has changed in character, become more sombre and severe. You are trying on clothes, and consider how they look on you and how they make you look. You are listening to a talk, and contrast the banality of what the speaker is saying with the pleasant tones and well chosen words in which he says it. You are playing a piece of music and it seems to carry you away. You are bedding out plants and try to get the spacing even or the colours well grouped. You admire the unhurried sureness of an elderly labourer's movements as he scythes or builds a dry stone wall. It strikes you that the postman has a funny face. Aesthetic judgement is exercised most formally, perhaps, in art galleries, concert halls and the like, but our lives would be very dull if it was in perpetual abeyance outside these temples dedicated to the muses.

I am suggesting that a vast and variegated throng of judgements may press forward, claiming to be aesthetic. Many theorists have felt that this cannot be allowed. They have tried to fix precise conditions for what is to count as an aesthetic judgement, and thus reduce *bona fide* aesthetic judgements to a homogeneous, easily managed group. One way of doing this is to argue that there is one single feature (or at most two or three such features) constituting aesthetic merit. All genuine aesthetic assessment is then assessment by the one genuinely aesthetic criterion: does the thing before us possess this feature? Clive Bell[1] took this line. He called the essential feature significant form, and held that unless a judgement is to the effect that something has or lacks significant form it is not an aesthetic judgement at all. Similarly many would say that to judge a thing aesthetically is, and can only be, to judge it as an expression of emotion.

Again, it has been thought that the mark of a genuine aesthetic judgement is that it is made in a special frame of mind: usually one of idleness, detachment, disinterestedness or passive receptivity. We suspend our natural sense of purpose and significance,[2] or instead of observing it and considering what qualities it has, we 'prehend' it and consider what 'aspects' 'animate' it.[3]

It has also been claimed that an aesthetic judgement is one with certain formal features which differentiate it from other sorts of judgement. Perhaps it is less conceptual in character; or it is related differently to the considerations we bring forward to support it. It in no way follows from these, and they do not function as proofs or even as reasons for accepting it, but rather as aids by which others may come to see or feel for themselves that it is right. Professor F. Sibley seems to adopt this approach. He places no restriction on the number of features which may be ascribed in a genuine aesthetic judgement; he offers an impressively rich vocabulary of expressions for them: 'unified, integrated, lifeless, serene, sombre, dynamic, powerful, vivid, delicate, moving, trite, sentimental, tragic, graceful, dainty, handsome, comely, elegant, garish' etc. But all genuinely

[1]Superior figures refer to Notes and Bibliography pp. 121–32.

aesthetic judgements, he thinks, have this in common, that they are reached by the exercise of a peculiar sort of intuition, which he hopes to characterise by comparing and contrasting it with our ability to discriminate colours.[4]

Some writers, of course, have employed all these methods of marking off a set of pure aesthetic judgements. The best example is Kant. Kant held that a judgement, to be aesthetic, must be on one of precisely two features, beauty and sublimity, both of which he defined very narrowly; he also held that it must have a peculiar freedom and disinterestedness; and he laid down for it certain formal conditions which I shall not go into, but which, the reader may take my word for it, are extremely stringent and technical.[5]

Today the opinion is gaining ground that all these efforts are misguided: that there is no single feature which makes a situation aesthetic, no single set of criteria by which we can recognise aesthetic judgements.[6] And that seems to be right. Certainly as soon as we have worked out our definition or laid down our limitations we shall find we have excluded cases we want to discuss—and a great many more cases which other people want to discuss, and which will not get considered if not by the aesthetician. Suppose I like adventure stories, and like them because they give me a thrill, because they carry me along and hold me in suspense. I may want to know what happens to me when I get carried along, how a story can thrill me, even, perhaps, what a story is or what it is that thrills. You simply exasperate me if you say that adventure stories and the enjoyment of them are no concern of the aesthetician: they are my concern, and I have turned to aesthetics for light on them. The aesthetician should rather go where there is work for him to do, than sit on Parnassus waiting for problems prepared to his specifications.

It may be thought, nevertheless, that aesthetic judgements must have something in common, since otherwise we would not call them all aesthetic. Bell's aesthetic theory starts from a similar idea: 'Either all works of art', he says, 'have some common quality, or when we speak of "works of art" we gibber'.[1] This way of thinking rests on a narrow theory about the meaning of words, the theory that the same word can be used of a number of different things only if there is some definite characteristic which those things all share, some clear-cut concept under which they all fall. (Where we seem to have an exception, as with the word 'pen', it can be said that we really have to do not with one word but two: the word 'pen' which we use for what we write with comes from the Latin 'penna', and the word 'pen' which we use for what we keep sheep in comes from Old English.)

It is hard to deny that there are some words which are used in the way described; so, perhaps, 'spherical', 'clove-hitch', 'kedge', 'oolite'. But there are plenty of other ways in which a word can be used without disintegrating like 'pen'. Followers of Wittgenstein have emphasised that the application of the same word to a number of different things may be grounded on what they call a family resemblance. A family resemblance (in the technical sense) holds between several things if each of them has a reasonable number of some set of characteristics; there need be no characteristic in the set which they all have, and the set itself need not be clearly delimited: we can add further characteristics if it becomes convenient to do so. The group of things is held together by a complicated pattern of overlapping and intersecting resemblances, rather as a rope is held together by the friction of many small fibres, even though there is no single fibre running its whole length. It is often claimed that games form a group of this sort. There is no one feature which all games have in common, but each game has a certain amount in common with several others. If you consider championship chess and backroom poker by themselves, it may seem odd to use the same word 'game' of them both; but it becomes intelligible when we see some of the chains linking them, for instance ordinary chess—draughts—backgammon—cribbage—piquet.[7]

This account of how the same expression may come to be applied to many very heterogeneous things, seems to work well for the expression 'aesthetic judgement'. Our attention to a shell beside us on the beach may seem very different from our attention to a performance of Bach's *Matthew Passion* in a cathedral, so long as we consider the two alone; but we can trace many paths between them when we look at the intervening territory, with other kinds of music, patterns of sound, paintings which involve shells, shell decorations in houses, literary allusions, mythology and so on. There is a group of judgements, attitudes, pleasures, activities, held together, not by some single thread running through them all, but by a web of limited resemblances and affinities, and these are the business of the aesthetician.

2. *Aesthetics and philosophy*

If aesthetics is the study of the things we assess aesthetically, and of our aesthetic assessment of them, what contribution has philosophy to make to it? The philosopher is not an art historian, or even a historian of taste. His aesthetic discriminations are no finer than those of other men. He has no special mission or eloquence to lead us to deeper or more subtle modes of aesthetic appreciation. So had he not better hold his peace?

An obvious answer is that philosophy can make the same sort of contribution here as anywhere else. Anything of which we make a special study is liable to disclose a side or throw up a problem in the face of which our specialist knowledge is useless; and the philosopher is not a man with a subject of his own, but rather a man who makes a speciality of dealing with that aspect of other people's subject matter, with which their expert knowledge does not help them to deal. It is true that cries for philosophical assistance are more often heard from some fields than from others; but aesthetics seems to be one from which they are (or philosophers may feel they should be) clear and incessant. A glance at two or three problems which will be treated more amply later will show what I mean.

Some aestheticians have held that aesthetics is primarily about art, and about products of nature such as flowers and mountains only insofar as we adopt an attitude to them like our attitude to works of art.[8] This needs arguing, since at first it looks arbitrary, but certainly very many things we assess aesthetically are works of art, or at least made or done by men. An important question, then, for the aesthetician is: what is a work of art? And this is not, at least in one aspect, a question for the art-expert. Examples of works of art are Beethoven's *Fifth Symphony*, the *Odyssey*, the *Mona Lisa*. Now many things we have to do with, such as our friends and relations, our dogs and slippers, are physical objects occupying places for times. Perhaps the *Mona Lisa* is such an object, but it is hard to say the same of Beethoven's *Fifth Symphony*, hard to say what place the *Odyssey* is occupying just now. Are works of art, then, qualities or dispositions of physical objects, like my arthritis or the shape of your nose? Or are they entities of a different sort altogether, like Platonic ideas? We have got into a difficulty from which we cannot be liberated by any knowledge of the intricacies of German music or Homeric syntax. The scholar is as helpless as the layman, and both must look to the philosopher. It may be added that the philosopher need not assume that works of art are all things of the same logical type: I shall in fact discuss separately what we mean by a picture, a piece of music and a poem.

Again, many works of art are representations, and since the time of Plato[9] it has been recognised that our experience of representations is not easy to analyse coherently. When we look at the *Mona Lisa*, do we see a woman? A real woman? A woman that is really there? Or a woman that is not really there? The *Odyssey* describes encounters with giants and sorceresses. But no such encounters ever took place. How can one describe an encounter that never took place, or distinguish it from another encounter which also never took place?

A literary critic might dismiss these last questions as frivolous, but others are perhaps more disturbing. Critics try to expound the meaning of works of literature, but the meaning at a deep and elusive level. In one way the meaning of a piece of writing is not a matter for dispute. If you produce a correct literal translation of a French poem, you show you know the meaning of the French, and people who know both French and English will not dispute about whether your translation is correct. But if you offer a critical interpretation of a French poem, whether you have grasped its meaning in another sense will be disputable. You yourself can argue for your interpretation in a way it would be vain to argue for your translation; and though there are people considered qualified to judge, an accurate knowledge of French and English is not thought to be their sole qualification. These people are of course the critics; and they may find it awkward to say just what their qualifications are,[10] or provide an exact characterisation of the kind of meaning with which they are concerned. Now the distinguishing and classifying of ways in which words and speeches can have meaning is a task for philosophers, and one to which they have in fact given much attention in recent years; I shall suggest in Chapter 5 that the results they have achieved may be used to shed light on obscure facets of the critic's activity.

That the problems just reviewed are suitable for philosophical treatment, perhaps nobody will deny; but it may be thought that they are, after all, peripheral. They all bear rather on the things we assess aesthetically than on our assessment of them, and since the eighteenth century, when people first started writing full-length books on aesthetics and the name itself was introduced (it was introduced by Baumgarten in 1750; before that, discussions like the present had no special name), it is on the grounds of aesthetic judgement and the nature of aesthetic experience that aestheticians have chiefly concentrated. The controversial question is whether philosophers have much to say on these topics. One reason for thinking not is that most philosphers who have tried their hands at them have made a disappointing showing. But it may also be feared that this poor success is inevitable, that aesthetic experience and judgement are by nature such that any prolonged philosophising about them is bound to be useless and dull.[11]

I hope it will eventually emerge that these fears are too pessimistic. They are not, however, entirely baseless. If we take up certain positions on two or three issues which are not proper to aesthetics but belong to philosophy generally, we shall indeed find, when we come to aesthetics, that we have left ourselves very little to say. These positions were orthodox in the eighteenth century, and have been effectively questioned only recently. They were accepted by nearly all writers on aesthetics, and such dreariness as hangs over the subject may, I think, be traced directly to their acceptance. Let me try to say what they are.

The most important concerns the notion of pleasure. It was supposed that pleasures are objects of awareness distinct from, and more or less on all fours with, other objects of awareness like sounds, patches of colour, heat and cold; and feeling pleasure or being pleased is being aware of a pleasure. We may say, if we like, that according to this view 'pleasure' is the name of a sensation, but if we say this we must understand by a sensation something which can be felt or 'perceived' by the mind, so that 'hot', 'cold', 'the sound of a trumpet' are also names of sensations. If we want to know further what a pleasure is, it is no use asking for a verbal description, since the word 'pleasure' stands for something simple and unanalysable, a 'simple idea': the only way of learning what a pleasure is like, is by having one. As Locke puts it, pleasure and pain 'like other simple ideas, cannot be described, nor their names defined: the way of knowing them is, as of the simple ideas of the senses, only by experience.'[12]

Although pleasures are thus, so to speak, independent objects of awareness, they come to us, it was held, along with other sensations. 'The infinitely wise Author of our being', as Locke piously expresses it, 'has been pleased to join to several thoughts and several sensations a perception of *delight*'.[13] In other words, a feeling of pleasure tends to be the accompaniment of something like tasting honey, or kissing a pretty girl, or hearing that you have won a lottery. We may say if we like that in these cases the pleasure is *caused* by the honey, girl or news, or by the sensations of tasting, kissing or hearing; but to say this, according to eighteenth-century theories of causality, is to say no more than that a sensation of pleasure is a normal or regular attendant of these other experiences. Hume in a famous passage defines a cause as 'an object precedent and contiguous to another, and where all objects resembling the former are placed in a like relation of priority and contiguity to those objects that resemble the latter',[14] and this definition would be accepted as basically sound by many today. Hence even if eighteenth-century writers hold that pleasure is causally connected with perceiving certain things, the connection they allow is still, in a sense, contingent. It is, for them, just an observed matter of fact that honey arouses pleasure and codliver oil disgust. There is no *logical* connection between pleasures and the things perception of which they attend. It is not a logical or conceptual necessity that we should be pleased when we hear we have won a lottery, or feel pain when someone runs a pin into us. It is logically possible for anything to give pleasure and for anything to give pain.

The consequences of this view of pleasure for aesthetics are obvious. One group of pleasures is the group of aesthetic pleasures— for although pleasures are all simple and unanalysable, they still differ, as do colours: 'under the term *pleasure* we comprehend sensations which are very different from each other, and which have only such a distant resemblance, as is requisite to make them be expressed by the same abstract term'.[15] (Hume, it will be noticed, accepts the narrow theory of meaning described above.) The task of the aesthetician, then, is simply to search out and classify the things perception of which is in fact accompanied by aesthetic pleasure. This was, indeed, recognised by early aestheticians. Hutcheson says at the beginning of his *Enquiry*: 'In the following papers, the word 'beauty' is taken for the idea raised in us, and "a sense of beauty" for our power of receiving this idea. "Harmony" also denotes our pleasant ideas arising from compositions of sounds, and "a good ear" (as it is generally taken), a power of receiving this pleasure. In the following sections an attempt is made to discover what is the *immediate occasion* of these pleasant ideas, or what real quality in the objects ordinarily excites them.'[16] Similarly Burke: the confusions about aesthetics prevalent in his day can find a remedy only 'from a diligent examination of our passions in our own breast; from a careful survey of the properties of things which we find by experience to induce those passions; and from a sober and attentive investigation of the laws of nature by which those properties are capable of affecting the body, and thus of exciting our passions'.[17]

An aesthetician working along these lines can explain our aesthetic pleasures in a way, but only in the way in which a doctor can explain what happens when we eat various things. The doctor can point out that some substances are in fact poisonous and others nutritious; he can group poisons and vitamin-bearing foods under a limited number of heads; and he can account for your throes last night by showing that they fall under a general law concerning strong alkalis and stomach tissues. But while he can thus provide an excuse for your groans, he cannot provide a reason for them: he cannot, I mean, make it seem any more reasonable to be poisoned by strychnine than by porridge, or explain the harm that comes to you by showing that there would be a logical awkwardness about thriving on the former. In the same way the aesthetician can group various works of art and pleasing or displeasing products of nature under various heads, and may try to account for your raptures over Botticelli's *Birth of Venus* by showing that they fall under a general law relating wavy shapes, colour combinations and human eyes; but again he renders them rather excusable than intelligible. He cannot make it seem any more reasonable to like this picture than any other, or explain your satisfaction by showing that there would be some logical awkwardness in giving the descriptions you would give of it, and at the same time declaring you find it an aesthetic flop.

So long, then, as he accepts an eighteenth-century view of pleasure, there is very little a philosopher can contribute to aesthetics. The grounds of an aesthetic judgement about a thing, he will have to say, are not something in the thing, but pleasant or unpleasant sensations in us; its character is one of extreme subjectivity; to claim that a thing has aesthetic merit is to say that you have certain feelings when you contemplate it—or, better, to betray or 'evince' those feelings; and for the rest, he will hand us over to the psychologist and sociologist to 'show us what in general are the causes of aesthetic feeling, why various societies produced and admired the works of art they did, why taste varies as it does within a given society, and so forth'. All this, as Professor A. J. Ayer has shown, can be done in a single paragraph.[18]

We may notice that conversely anyone who thinks that aesthetic judgement is irreducibly subjective had better accept the eighteenth-century view of pleasure. It is natural enough to take the line that our aesthetic enjoyments are a highly personal and private affair, that our tastes are what we like, and so on. But if we think that it is not merely impertinent but senseless to ask a man to defend his aesthetic preferences or say why he likes what he likes, that must be because of our conception of what it is to like something; and what can this conception be but that liking is a matter of having an eighteenth-century sensation?

As I intimated, the eighteenth-century account of pleasure has lately come under heavy fire[19]. Although it is allowed that there are sensations which are pleasant, many arguments are brought to show that pleasures generally are not sensations. For instance a sensation is usually locatable in some part of your body: you feel an itch or pain in your foot; while most pleasures are not so locatable: *As you like it* does not give you a pleasure in your eyes. Sensations are things such as we find pleasant or unpleasant, enjoy or do not enjoy having; it sounds odd to talk of a pleasure being pleasant or enjoyed. We can be wrong or in doubt about what is causing a sensation, but we are not in doubt about what we are taking pleasure in. And on the positive side pleasure is explained in a way I shall try to indicate in Chapter 2, according to which the connection between pleasure and its objects is not so much causal as logical. If that is correct there will be room for discussion about whether a thing is apt to please and how it comes to be pleasing independent of the reports of individuals that they have felt certain sensations; and though we shall not be able to prove to someone that something pleases him when he thinks it does not, we may be able to suggest reasons why it does not please him, and aesthetic satisfactions will no longer be unanalysable, or wholly incapable of justification.

Another philosophical topic on which an aesthetician may adopt an unlucky view is emotion. In the eighteenth century very much the same account was given of emotions as of pleasure. Anger, fear and the like were held to be feelings which we know by feeling them; they cannot be described with any accuracy, and though they accompany other experiences—fear, for instance, might accompany seeing an approaching lion—they are related only contingently to the experiences they accompany. We may say, if we like, that the lion, or the sight of it, causes our fear; but we must recognise that there is no logical connection between fear and what we say we are afraid of. It is logically possible for anything to give rise to any emotion. Further, though a person feeling a given emotion will normally behave in a certain way—a person feeling fear, for instance, may turn pale or tremble—still, there is at best only a contingent causal connection between an emotion and the behaviour which we say is the expression of it. It is logically possible for grief to give rise to swearing and stamping about, for terror to find its outward manifestation in sighs and silent tears, for suicide to be an expression of *joie de vivre*, and in general for anything to be the expression of any emotion.[20]

Now it is a widely held aesthetic theory that a thing has aesthetic merit insofar as it expresses (or communicates, or something of that sort) emotion. In Chapter 4 I shall discuss how this theory can best be developed; but clearly it cannot be made to work at all, so long as we accept the eighteenth-century account of emotions. Suppose I claim that a particular work of art results from a particular emotion on the part of the artist, or inspires a particular emotion in me. The first claim will have to be established historically, from evidence about the artist's life; the second runs into technical difficulties in that it may be doubted whether a man's declaration that he himself has a certain feeling, should be regarded as a *bona fide* statement at all. (When I make a genuine statement, it seems it must be possible for me to be mistaken; but how can I be mistaken about my present emotional state? Perhaps while statements are true or false, my declaraction that this poem moves me in a certain way is rather truthful or deceitful.) And even if my claims are allowed, they do not take us any further, since anything else could have been the expression of the same emotion in the artist or the cause of the same emotion in me, and the same work of art could equally have resulted from, and caused, quite different emotions.

If many discussions about the emotional content and impact of works of art seem sterile and inconclusive, the explanation is not far to seek. Neither is the remedy. It lies in a better account of the emotions, such as may be found in any supermarket (if I may so describe the learned periodicals) of contemporary philosophy.

It is fairly obvious that our views on pleasure and emotion will have an effect on our aesthetics. The same holds, though the effect may be less far-reaching, for perception, and here too the influence of eighteenth century philosophical thought has been unfortunate.

At the beginning of the eighteenth century it was supposed that perception in general is a matter of receiving mental images or representations of things, and when a man is said to see, for example, a bowl of fruit on the table, what really happens is that light rays stimulate his optic nerves, and as a consequence a two-dimensional image comes before his mind, which is exactly like a *trompe l'oeil* picture of a bowl of fruit on the table. Thus Locke says: 'When we set before our eyes a round globe of any uniform colour, e.g. gold, alabaster or jet, it is certain that the idea thereby implanted on our mind is of a flat circle variously shadowed, with several degrees of light and brightness coming to our eyes. . . . The idea we receive from thence is only a plane variously coloured, *as is evident in painting*'[21] (my italics).

If we accept this account of vision (and it has in fact enjoyed, at least among artists, a long and eventful innings), the task of the painter of representative pictures is straightforward: he has simply to copy what he sees. Ruskin provides a classic statement: 'Everything that you can see in the world around you, presents itself to your eyes only as an arrangement of patches of different colours variously

shaded. . . . We *see* nothing but flat colours. . . . The whole art of
painting consists merely in perceiving the shape and depth of these
patches of colour, and putting patches of the same size, depth and
shape on canvas.'[22] It may be added that anyone who wishes
seriously to maintain that artists should or can paint pictures by
copying what they see, will do well to hold that what we see are
mental pictures. For as the word 'copy' is ordinarily used, we copy
what we see when we do likewise. Attending an unfamiliar religious
service, you might copy the people you see around you, kneel when
they kneel etc. How one would set about copying a mountain or a
tree is a difficult question. We do, however, talk of copying pictures;
people may sometimes be seen at it in public art galleries; and if all
representative painting is to be called copying what we see, what we
see must be supposed to be always a mental picture of some sort.

In fact, however, it is very inconvenient to give this sort of account
of representation, since as Professor E. H. Gombrich has shown at
length in *Art and illusion*, we will then be unable to explain the
enormous differences in style exhibited by painters in different
ages and societies. Byzantine, Chinese and seventeenth-century
western European artists had all much the same command of their
tools and materials. They paint much the same things, trees, hills,
animals and so on. If they simply copied the mental pictures they
received, why are their actual pictures so different? It seems absurd to
suppose they received different mental images.[23]

As the eighteenth century proceeded, philosophers began to feel
the naivity of saying that in ordinary vision we receive mental images
which are just like physical pictures except that they are mental.
The opinion gained ground that what we receive are only fragmentary,
disconnected sensations, and out of these we ourselves build up the
perceptible world as we normally think of it. This line of speculation
culminates in Kant. Kant held that the raw materials we receive are
so raw that by themselves they cannot even be recognised as sensations, cannot even be objects of conscious awareness at all: anything
of which we are consciously aware is already a construction put
together by our imaginative powers. He also argued that there are
certain very basic and general patterns or schemata, according to
which we have to order any sensory intake if we are to have an object
of which we can be conscious. Kant's philosophy of perception is
generally reckoned difficult, but the difference between him and
Locke may perhaps be illustrated well enough for our purposes as
follows. When we order a boat, doll's house or television set from a
distant shop, it may arrive ready assembled or needing only a

minimum of setting up; or our parcel may contain a lot of screws and struts, and a blue-print for doing it ourselves. Locke thought that we receive ready-assembled images of a perceptible world; Kant held that we get screws and struts, or rather not even that but a load of iron ore. What we construct out of this is not so much a picture of the external world as the external world itself. And the most important blueprints we possess are those for smelting the ore into stuff we can work with.

Kant's theory had considerable influence on subsequent aesthetics. Kant himself, in his *Critique of aesthetic judgement*, argues that a beautiful object is one the sensory materials for which are particularly easy for the imagination to penetrate and form: 'It is easy to conceive that the object may supply ready-made to the imagination just such a form of the manifold as the imagination, if it were left to itself, would freely project'[24]—rather as if our load of ore were to contain a gold nugget the exact shape of a shirt-stud. Coleridge suggested that poetic creativity is just an extension and heightened form of the Kantian imagination's ordinary constructive activity.[25] The expressionist aesthetic theory of Croce and Collingwood depends, as we shall see, on an identification of intuition, representation and expression, which is plausible only on a Kantian view of what is involved in ordinary perceptual experience. And most recently Mrs S. Langer has put forward a philosophy of art the Kantian basis of which is obvious and admitted:

Our merest sense experience is a process of *formulation*. The world that actually meets our senses is not a world of 'things' . . .; the world of pure sensation is so complex, so fluid and full, that sheer sensitivity to stimuli would encounter what William James has called . . . 'A blooming, buzzing confusion'. Out of this bedlam, our sense organs must select certain predominant forms, if they are to make report of *things* and not of mere dissolving sensa. The eye and the ear must have their logic—their 'categories of understanding', if you like the Kantian idiom, or their 'primary imagination' in Coleridge's version of the same concept. An object is not a datum, but a form construed by the sensitive and intelligent organ, a form which is at once an experienced individual thing and a symbol for the concept of it, for *this sort of thing*. . . . The fundamental materials given to our senses, the *Gestalten* or fundamental perceptual forms . . . belong to the 'presentational' order. They furnish the elementary abstractions in terms of which ordinary sense experience is understood. This kind of understanding is directly reflected in the pattern of *physical reaction*, impulse and instinct. May not the order of perceptual forms, then, be a possible principle for symbolisation, and hence the conception, expression and apprehension, of impulsive, sentient life?[26]

Faced by any theory of this kind, we ought to ask: what precisely are these forms which are supposed to impart aesthetic value to things or render them expressive? And how are we to recognise their presence? Two sorts of answer seem possible. First, it might be said that experimental psychology has revealed, or will some day soon reveal, certain forms which we endeavour to find in our fields of vision, certain principles of grouping which we try out before others. This does not sound implausible; nor is it implausible that things which exemplify these forms or can be grouped according to these principles, should be aesthetically pleasing. However, there remains the question why they are pleasing, since most of those who are pleased will never have heard of these forms or principles, and cannot, therefore, be pleased *that* they are present or apply. And further, it is hard to see how this sort of account can cover more than a small group of cases, chiefly cases where we are pleased by some fairly simple abstract design.

Most of the aestheticians of whom I am speaking, including Kant himself, would hesitate to lean at all heavily on empirical psychology. The basic schemata for sense-experience, they would say, are too basic and too universal to be discovered empirically. And they cannot be described in scientific or 'discursive' language. On the contrary, the whole point of the theory is that it is only in art, by the infinitely varied and subtle symbolism of the various arts, that they can be captured and conveyed. Now whether or not this answer is to our taste, this way lies mysticism. We have left the realm of rational argument. And it is clear where we left it: we left it with Kant's account of perception and experience. His initial insight, that to be conscious of a thing at all we must be aware of it as satisfying some concept, is sound and valuable, but his development of this is pure fantasy. A recent commentator has called it a transcencental drama; none of the *dramatis personae*, neither the raw sensations, nor the Kantian imagination, nor the basic schemata, nor the 'categories of the pure understanding' mentioned by Mrs Langer, bear any resemblance, or seem to have any relation, to anything we encounter in the real world.

I have tried to show that the idea that philosophy has little to contribute to aesthetics, itself derives from fairly extensive philosophising. Those who have found that aesthetic experience and judgement lie beyond the reach of words and rational argument, have themselves excluded them by philosophical decisions on the topics I have been reviewing, pleasure, emotion and perception. One obvious service philosophy can do aesthetics is to revoke those decisions, offer accounts of the crucial topics which will permit aesthetic debate to get under way.

But whether we give our permission or not, aesthetic debate does in fact take place and will continue. It is clear that people talk over the merits of books, pictures, bits of landscape and so forth, and attention will show that consciously or unconsciously they make use of various standards and criteria. There seems no reason why even a philosopher who thinks that aesthetic taste is ultimately subjective should not try to elicit these criteria and discuss problems about formulating and applying them. Even if they are not in practice applied rigorously, if it is characteristic of aesthetic debate not to press points too hard, and to place success rather in arguing well than in forcing an opponent to submit, the philosopher may hope to shed some light on what is at issue and what a good argument is. In the next three chapters I shall in fact examine three types or groups of criteria which I think people discussing aesthetic merit have wished to employ; and I shall consider both general questions about pleasure, emotion and the like, and specific problems about works of art and other things we assess aesthetically as they arise in connection with these.

2

PURE FORM

1. *Formalist criteria*

'As music is the poetry of sound', said Whistler, 'so is painting the poetry of sight, and the subject-matter has nothing to do with harmony of sound or of colour. The great musicians knew this. Beethoven and the rest wrote music—simply music; symphony in this key, concerto or sonata in that. On F or G they constructed celestial harmonies—as harmonies—as combinations, evolved from the chords of F or G and their minor correlatives. . . . Art should be independent of all clap-trap—should stand alone, and appeal to the artistic sense of eye or ear, without confounding this with emotions entirely foreign to it, as devotion, pity, love, patriotism, and the like. All these have no kind of concern with it and that is why I insist on calling my works "arrangements" and "harmonies".'[1]

Whistler is here asking us to judge his pictures by what may be called formalist criteria: we should attend to the pure forms exhibited in them, to the exclusion of their subject matter, their emotive suggestions and the rest. Some aestheticians have held that this is the only truly aesthetic way of assessing anything. That, on the face of it, seems hardly reasonable. Works of literature, which we want to assess aesthetically, do not embody any pure forms comparable to those we might find in a Beethoven symphony, and even if all pictures do, they are not the only things to which we attend when we look at a picture by Giotto or Goya. Still, formalist criteria are in some ways simpler or more elementary than other criteria of aesthetic appraisal, and we may begin by looking at some of the problems to which their formulation and application give rise; for the task of separating off considerations of pure form from all others is not quite so straightforward as Whistler's words might suggest.[2]

Take, for instance, Clive Bell's theory of significant form. All works of art worthy of the name, thought Bell, have something in common. What is that? 'Only one answer seems possible: significant form. In each, lines and colours combined in a particular way, certain forms and relations of forms, stir our aesthetic emotions. These relations and combinations of lines and colours, these aesthetically moving forms, I call "Significant Form".'[3] And having said this, Bell thinks he has given an exposition of his view sufficient for the purposes of the aesthetician. We can, however, obtain further insight into what he takes significant form to be, from his account of how the artist looks at things. 'Occasionally, when an artist looks at objects (the contents of a room, for instance) he perceives them as pure forms in certain relations to each other, and feels emotion for them as such. . . . Now to see objects as pure forms is to see them as ends in themselves. . . . Having seen it [the object] as pure form, having freed it from all casual and adventitious interest, from all that it may have acquired from its commerce with human beings, from all its significance as a means, he [the artist] has felt its significance as an end in itself.'[4] Kant spoke of treating men as ends in themselves, and meant by that treating them as autonomous agents with an inalienable right to our respect. Bell, it is clear, has something quite different in mind. For him, seeing a man as an end in himself would be seeing him simply as a combination of lines and colours, or, in short, as pattern; and if a work of art is to succeed, it will succeed, we may infer, as a pattern, and not as a representation or as something with some function or relation to men or other living things.

While Bell's theory remains in this state of virgin simplicity it is attractive: it does seem possible for a work of art, such as a Persian rug or Baroque confessional, and also for a natural object or phenomenon like a shell or sunset, to succeed as a pattern. But Bell promptly falls from grace by reintroducing non-formal considerations which we shall find typical of theological aesthetics. He would have liked to say that the artist finds his inspiration simply in the pure forms of objects around him; but musicians, potters and the like produce genuine works of art, and it is hard to point to visible objects whose pure forms they have been contemplating. So Bell is forced to suppose that inspiration comes, not from lines and colours themselves, but from 'reality which reveals itself through line and colour . . . It would follow that significant form was form behind which we catch a sense of ultimate reality. . . . The emotions which artists feel . . . that many of us feel when we contemplate works of art . . . would be emotions felt for reality revealing itself through pure forms.'[4]

Bell in practice confined himself to works of visual art, though he thought that his account could be extended to music. Mrs Langer took up the challenge. 'Music', she justly observes 'is preeminently non-representative even in its classical productions, its highest attainments. It exhibits pure form not as an embellishment, but as its very essence; we can take it in its flower—for instance, German music from Bach to Beethoven—and have practically nothing but tonal structures before us: no scene, no object, no fact.'[5] And she endeavours to show that 'music is "Significant Form" in the peculiar sense of "significant" which Mr Bell and Mr Fry maintain they can grasp or feel, but not define'. In the course of her attempt, however, she has to abandon the position that music is non-representative. It is, she says (her italics), '*formulation and representation* of emotions, moods, mental tensions and resolutions—a "logical picture" of sentient, responsive life.' She uses the expression 'logical picture' to put us in mind of the view, developed by Wittgenstein in the *Tractatus*, that a proposition is a logical picture of a fact. Pictures in general, to be pictures, have to have certain formal features in common with what they represent. An ordinary picture can represent an ordinary scene because the patches of paint have spatial relations the same as, or answering to, the spatial relations of things in the real scene. Those who tried to explain propositions as logical pictures claimed that a proposition shares logical form with the fact it represents—by logical form being meant what formal logicians study. Mrs Langer does not think that music shares logical form in this strict sense with emotions and moods; but she claims that it exhibits patterns of motion, rest, sudden change and so on which are also exhibited by electrical processes in the brain; or, alternatively, by intellectual and emotional processes as known by introspection; or, perhaps, which are the patterns (see above p. 20) which we impose on sense-impressions generally in order to have conscious experience. Music is thus logically fitted to be a symbolism or language. It differs, however, from ordinary languages, on the one hand in that it 'articulates forms which language cannot set forth', and on the other in that it is, so to speak, only the formal apparatus for representing emotional life: the same piece of music can be used by different hearers or on different occasions as a vehicle for the conception or intuition of different emotions; in this way the elements in a piece of music are rather like algebraical symbols or functions in the mathematical sense than like numerals: a piece of music might be compared with $2(\ )^3 + (\ )$, which we can fill in with our own arguments.

Mrs Langer's account is open to various objections. As was said above, in making music represent what cannot be described in speech, she removes her claim that it represents from the realm of discussion in speech. We must also be disturbed by her uncertainty about what it is—whether brain processes, introspected moods or Kantian schemata—that music shares a form with, particularly as all three candidates have drawbacks. And it is unclear that there could be a symbolism at once as precise and as fluid as she claims music to be: certainly the mathematical analogy is hard to work out convincingly in any detail. Instead, however, of pressing these difficulties, let us see whether it is necessary to give up the search for purely formalist criteria and bring in representation or symbolism at all. Perhaps we can show how pieces of music and patterns can succeed simply as pieces of music and patterns. The first step in this enquiry must be to say precisely what pieces of music and patterns are.

2. *Music and patterns*

What is a piece of music? A good deal has lately been written on this, and the general verdict is that Beethoven's *Fifth Symphony*, for instance, is not the ink-marks made by Beethoven on pieces of paper, or any of the printed music currently used by performers, nor is it any or all of the performances which have been or will be given, but an entity which stands to these performances in the relation of type to token.[6]

The terms 'type' and 'token' were introduced by Pierce in the context of a discussion of signs[7], in order to distinguish a single word, e.g. the word 'the', from the numerous appearances of that word in a piece of writing or speech. The many printed 'the's on this page he called tokens of the type 'the', and he said that they stood to this type as instances of it. Recent writers extend the notion of a type to cover units of measurement such as a yard, tokens of which would be particular yardsticks and the like, so called cultural objects such as the 1965 Morris 1100, tokens of which would be the contents of your garage and mine, things like the Union Jack, tokens of which are particular expanses of cloth, and the references or things named by such names as *the Odyssey, God Save the Queen, the Mona Lisa*.

Types are distinguished on the one hand from paradigms, on the other from universals. To distinguish them from paradigms is clearly correct. A type may sometimes be related to a paradigm; thus the length a yard is the length perfectly instantiated or exemplified by a certain carefully chosen piece of metal; but still this piece of metal is not the type, but only a paradigmatic token of it. The distinction between types and universals is more doubtful. People want to draw it, because they want to say that works of art exist and come into being, but not that universals do either, and if works of art are types and type are universals, they will be in a fix. This, however, is only a motive for distinguishing types and universals; reasons are harder to find. Professor R. Wollheim takes universals to be entities the natural expressions for which are abstract, e.g. redness, and says that properties which belong to an instance of a universal because it is an instance of that universal, cannot belong to the universal, whereas properties which belong to a token because it is a token of a certain type, must belong to that type. Thus instances of redness are coloured, but redness is not; whereas tokens of the Union Jack are coloured and rectangular, and so is the type itself. Taking this line he is able to say that the distinction between, e.g. a piece of music and performances of it, hardly concerns the aesthetician, since 'anything which can be predicated of a performance of a piece of music can also be predicated of the piece of music itself'.

I do not find Wollheim's account very clear. At one point he says that both redness and its instances can be exhilarating, and while this is a natural way of speaking it seems to spoil his distinction. But more serious, his example of a universal is unrepresentative. I suppose he would allow that a pillar-box, insofar as it is red, is an instance of redness; of what is it an instance *qua* pillar-box? Of pillar-boxness? It is very artificial to introduce such an entity; the natural thing to say is that it is an instance of a pillar-box; and a pillar-box is something we might suppose to be a type. Abstract expressions are not in fact commonly used for things instantiated or exemplified, but for degrees of instantiation or exemplification. If I attracted or annoyed Chloe's femininity, I find her an attractively or annoyingly good example, not of femininity, but of a woman. For what is exemplified we use a concrete term, as for a type. As to Wollheim's example of a type, the Union Jack, how precisely does he conceive it? As a rectangular coloured object with no size or place? That sounds very odd. If it is red, white and blue, but still different from the universals red(ness), white(ness) and blue(ness), how does it differ? Is it a pattern, or way of distributing, red, white and blue? Patterns, colours, shapes, arrangements, they all sound logically similar: are none of them universals, or if some, why not the rest?

The distinction, then, between types and universals, seems to me unclear; but as a compromise, which I think illuminates the mode of existence of types, we may use the word 'possibility'. The relation of type to token is that of a possibility to a fulfilment of that possibility. We talk of the making of movements and gestures, the laughing of laughs etc.: the making of a movement stands to the movement made as fulfilment of a possibility to possibility fulfilled. The type word 'the' is a possible word, and its uses at various points in a speech or piece of writing are fulfilments of the possibility. Possibilities have the handy feature that one and the same possibility can be fulfilled a number of times or have a number of fulfilments, but they do not clutter up the universe: a possibility as such is a possibility, not something actual; it is fulfilments of possibilities that are actualities. The relation of a piece of music to performances of that piece is clearly the same as that of a journey to makings of that journey on different occasions or by different people, and so we may say that a piece of music, as contrasted with performances of it, is a possibility. Similarly a song is a possibility, and the singing of it a fulfilment of that possibility.

A particular journey, e.g. the journey from London to York, is a possible change of place. What kind of possibility is a piece of music, like the *Goldberg Variations*? A change in respect of sound on the part of a physical object, or, if the piece is for several instruments or voices, a set of physical objects. Physical objects such as pianos and the human larynx can be made to sound, and a sounding object may change in sound in at least three ways: loudness, pitch and quality or timbre. The human voice changes in timbre when it passes from one vowel sound to another, and a violin and a piano on which the same note is sounded with the same amplitude differ in timbre. Pieces of music are changes in sound in one or more of these ways, and names of pieces of music, like *the Goldberg Variations*, are names of changes in sound—names in the way in which 'a regular hexagon' 'a cylinder with the radius equal to the height' are names of shapes.

Musical composition is thinking up, or working out, a possible change in sound. A composer may be said to write down, in musical notation, a piece of music; but what he works out and writes down is strictly a *prescription* for a performance. Moral philosophers often talk as if prescriptions were much the same as orders and commands, but in ordinary speech we distinguish between orders and commands on the one hand, and prescriptions, formulae, sets of instructions and directions on the other. The doctor gives you a prescription for a cough-medicine, and you give the chemist an order for it. To give me instructions for getting from one place to another is to specify movements the making of which would be the making or going on of that journey. Bach wrote a prescription for the *Goldberg Variations* in that he specified the finger movements the making of which by a performer, or the changes in sound the undergoing of which by an instrument, is the going on or performance of the *Goldberg Variations*.

It should of course be recognised that the prescription or formula followed by the performer is not exclusively the composer's but partly his own.[8] That is particularly obvious with plainsong, since the notation is crude and limited; the individual choir-master or player lengthens and shortens notes, inserts pauses and so forth. But an experienced audience easily detects the difference between, say, Rosalyn Tureck's *Goldberg Variations* and Wanda Landowska's. Hence in just the way in which we can discuss the merits of the *Goldberg Variations*, and say it is one of Bach's better or worse pieces, we can discuss the merits of Rosalyn Tureck's *Goldberg Variations*: we do not just assess her digital nimbleness in following the formula, but we assess the formula she is following as if it were, as it is, in part her work.

The ontological status, then, of pieces of music, is fairly clear: they are definite, specific possibilities, which are fulfilled in performances. It is not appropriate to say that they have an interrupted existence in between performances, any more than it is appropriate to say that the existence of the Union Jack is interrupted between particular flags. A piece of music may be said, like any other possibility, to exist so long as it is a possibility. But is that not from all eternity? Not exactly. Some possibilities get fulfilled naturally, for instance movement in an elliptical orbit, the shape of a rhinoceros, and these, it might be said, are there already, and merely discovered by men. But others are fulfilled only through the purposive action of men; so, for instance, the combination of elements needed to make a delicious cake, or the change in sound undergone by a piano on which a sonata is played. Possibilities like these we do not so much discover as invent, and inasmuch as they can be fulfilled only through us, it might be said that they are possibilities, and hence exist, only so long as we retain prescriptions for fulfilling them; so that a sonata exists as long as someone knows or has the means of learning how to play it.

Not only pieces of music, but also works of visual art (and also works of literature, but we shall come to that in Chapter 5) have been called types; and insofar as they are or exemplify patterns, this seems reasonable. But if a type is a possibility, what sort of possibility is a pattern?

A piece of music is a change in sound which goes on through time. Similarly a journey from London to York goes on through time, and it might be thought at first that the same holds for all kinds of change; but in fact it is possible to speak of changes going on through space.

If you boil a kettle the water changes in temperature, let us say, by 50°C in five minutes. Now imagine a slab five feet long, which is 20°C at one end and 70°C at the other: it might be perfectly correct to say that it changes in temperature by 50°C in five feet. In the sense in which the water in the kettle changes temperature through time, the slab changes temperature through space. Similarly an object may change colour through time, as when a tomato ripens from green to red, or through space, like an apple which is green on one side and red on the other.

A pattern may be defined as a change through space in respect of visible qualities. Colour is not the only visible quality which can vary through space. Things vary in size through space; thus a dagger gets thinner throughout its length, or a road wider as it approaches the capital. And shapes generally may be regarded as variations through space. Thus a triangle may be regarded as the getting shorter and passing away of a horizontal line in so many units of height.

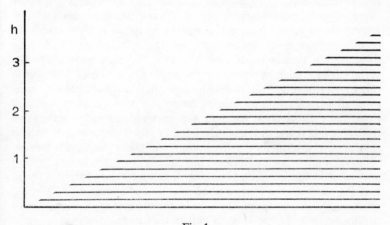

Fig. 1

Again, the movement of a point at a distance from another point, i.e. in a circle, may be reckoned in units of length, and a point may change direction by so many degrees of arc, not just in a certain time, but in a certain number of units measured along its path. Any picture, representative or abstract, exemplifies variations in colour and size extending over its surface area, and the artist who is planning a picture is working out such a variation or pattern. Similarly an architect, sculptor or interior decorator works out patterns: in an imposing house, for instance, there are variations in height and depth extending across the facade. And natural objects like shells instantiate patterns.

Mrs Langer notices what I call changes through space, but considers them illusory. She gives some pictures of decorative motifs and comments: 'Lines that intersect in a central point "emanate" from that centre, although they never actually change their relation to it. Similar or congruent elements "repeat" each other, colours "balance" each other, though they have no physical weight, etc. All these metaphorical terms denote relationships that belong to the virtual object, the created illusion. . . . The border is fixed on the surface whereon it is painted, printed, embroidered or carved . . . the "movement" of the border is not really movement in the scientific sense, change of place; it is semblance of rhythm.'[9]

Mrs Langer's remarks are not very consistent. Why does she use inverted commas for 'emanate' but not for 'intersect'? 'Intersect' is just as much a verb of action as 'emanate'; so is the verb, not easily dispensable in discussions of shape, 'curve'. But her chief mistake, I think, is to make changes through space illusions. A variation in colour through space differs from one through time in that it may itself be the terminal point of a change through time. Thus the variation in colour exhibited by the apple is the end of a temporal process of ripening. Still, true statements may be made about changes through space exactly parallel to statements about changes through time. We may say that the slab rises in temperature by 50° in five feet; that it is rising in temperature for five feet; and if it is correct to say, at any instant in the five minutes it takes the kettle to boil, 'The water is getting hotter now', it is equally correct to say, indicating any point in the five feet, 'The slab is getting hotter here'.

If the relation of a type to a token is that of a change to its going on through time or space, the type is not something over and above the token, but the position is rather that a single thing, a single change, can be considered in two ways, as a type or as a token, as a possible change or as the fulfilment of that possibility. A piece of music may be thought of as a change from one tone to another or from one degree of loudness to another; or it may be thought of as extending for so many minutes; in the former case we are thinking of it as a type, in the latter, as a token of that type. And similarly a work of visual art may be considered as a variation from one colour or size to another, or as a variation extending over so many square or cubic feet; in the one case it is thought of as a type, in the other as a token.

The advantage of this for us is that we avoid saying that types are extensive magnitudes, explain how it is that the Union Jack, though consisting of coloured triangles and crosses, does not extend for any distance or take up any part of the universe.

A composer feels he has done his job when he has written down a formula for others to follow in making instruments sound. The artist does not normally write down a formula to be followed in colouring expanses of canvas or chipping blocks of marble, but himself colours or chips in accordance with his formula. By a work of musical art we normally mean the possible change in sound; by a work of visual art we normally mean the execution or going on of a possible pattern: the *Goldberg Variations* are not a particular hour of variation in sound; a sunrise by Turner is a particular square yard or so of variation in colour. The musical type is defined by a written account, the score, while a painting type is defined by a paradigmatic token: Michelangelo's *Last Judgement qua* type or pattern is the pattern exemplified by the wall of the Sistine Chapel. These assymmetries are not surprising when we consider that a piece of music goes on through time where a pattern goes on through space; and once we have noticed them, there is no need to try to remove them by saying that the work of visual art is really the type and not the paradigmatic token. Sometimes by a work of visual art we do mean a type; so, perhaps, with Morris's 'chrysanthemum' pattern; but when we speak of well-known pictures, statues and buildings, we mean the paradigmatic token.

3. *Pleasure and pleasant sensations*

Having said what pieces of music and patterns are, we may enquire how, as such, they can be successful. Now it is so natural that it can hardly be wrong to say that a piece of music or pattern is a success if it gives pleasure, if it is pleasant to hear or look at. But here we meet the difficulty sketched in the first chapter: if 'pleasure' is the name of a sensation which anything may excite in anyone, it will be at best a psychological generalisation and not an aesthetic judgement to say that a certain object of sight or hearing is apt to please. To dispose of this doubt we need an alternative account of pleasure and sensation.

A modern approach to the notion of pleasure,[10] which seems both reasonable in itself and convenient for the aesthetician, is by way of pleasurable or enjoyable activity. Often when we experience pleasure we are taking pleasure in doing something. Now when we take pleasure in, or enjoy, playing bridge or gardening, we are not being

B

pleased by or enjoying anything extraneous to the activity, nor is our enjoyment itself an activity over and above the gardening or the Bridge. There are no extraneous objects of awareness, or if there are, attention to and enjoyment of them destroys our pleasure in the original activity; and if enjoying were an activity coordinate with gardening or bridge, we should have to keep switching from one to the other, and the sensible course would be to concentrate on enjoying ourselves and do nothing else; but this seems impossible, even for the very rich.

Enjoying Øing, then, or pleasure in Øing, is not something separable from Øing, but must rather be regarded as Øing in a certain way. But how? For two people, it appears, may both tend very similar garden patches in a similar manner, yet one experiences pleasure while the other does not. In the first place, a person who is enjoying Øing must know that he is Øing and have at least some idea how to Ø. Suppose a child has no knowledge of the difference between flowers and weeds, of the progression of the seasons, or of how to make a patch of ground look like a garden: the child is wrong to claim that he enjoys gardening; the most we can concede is that he enjoys wielding tools in the garden. Again, suppose I know that the sound of the gramophone keeps bad sleepers awake, and I play the gramophone all night, and you are kept awake: if I do not know that you are a bad sleeper or that you have taken the flat above, you cannot justly complain: 'He enjoys keeping me awake'.

Knowing how to Ø and knowing that you are Øing are prerequisites of Øing voluntarily: a Øer who satisfies them will normally be said to Ø voluntarily, unless the opposite can be shown. We may, however, strengthen the notion of Øing voluntarily by adding the condition that there should be some reason for Øing, known to the person who Øs. Reasons may be various in kind. If someone has asked you to make up a four at bridge, or if you will be paid for gardening, these are reasons. Some descriptions, of course, under which we know what we are doing, themselves embody reasons for doing it; so, perhaps, 'pulling a drowning man out of the water': it would usually be deemed a reason for pulling a man out of the water, that he is drowning.

It might be held that if a person is Øing voluntarily, then he is enjoying himself unless we can show otherwise: that is, we do not have to specify further conditions to be satisfied if he is to take pleasure in Øing, but the words 'pleasure', 'enjoy' etc. are so used that people are assumed to enjoy doing what they do voluntarily unless some special factor, e.g. an excruciating stomach-ache, a very recent bereavement, can be adduced which would explain their not enjoying it. But this seems inadequate. We voluntarily undergo hardships for the sake of some ulterior benefit, but do not always enjoy them.

At least two further conditions seem to be needed: that the person Øing should do so attentively, and that he should do what he does for its own sake, even if he also has other reasons which by themselves would be sufficient. What do I mean by doing something for its own sake? We sometimes say that a man does something for its own sake, if he does it for pleasure or for the pleasure of doing it, but we cannot say that here without circularity. We may approach the notion, however, of doing something for its own sake, by considering how we do something attentively.

In any activity which may be a pleasure you do a number of particular things, and if you are to do what you are doing well, these particular acts must be determined by factors so to speak internal to the activity. The point can best be brought out by an illustration: consider a game of bridge. To play bridge well is to play so as to win most and lose fewest points. In playing bridge you make bids and play cards. If you are to play well, what bid you make at any juncture, what card you play, must be determined by what cards you hold, and what other players have bid and played. You play attentively if you do what is right straight off, not by chance, but because of these factors, or if you take these factors into account in deliberating what to bid or play, even if you come to a wrong decision. Now suppose you are a defender with the lead, and your partner has bid spades. If you lead a spade because of this, that is, because he evidently holds some strength in the suit and leading it seems to offer the best chance of defecting the contract, and similarly at other junctures, you are playing bridge for the sake of playing bridge, even if you also have other objects. If you lead a spade not for such reasons, and against your judgement as a bridge player (perhaps your singleton diamond would be a better lead), but because your partner will be angry with you if you do not lead his suit, and it is the same throughout the game, you are not playing bridge for the sake of playing bridge. A way in which you can tell, is by whether it is easy, or requires an effort, to play attentively. If you already know what has been played, or if the fact that you have the lead seems to you a sufficient reason for trying to remember what has been played, and in this sense it is effortless to play attentively, you are playing bridge for the sake of playing bridge; but if you try to remember what has been played only because otherwise you will spoil the game for the others, or lose more than you can afford, you are not. It is fairly

obvious that if a person is playing bridge attentively for the sake of
playing bridge, in the sense indicated, he is likely to enjoy himself,
but otherwise not, unless, indeed he derives pleasure from gratifying
his partner, or the company, or the like.

Perhaps this sounds unnecessarily complicated. Does not a man
enjoy what he is doing if he is *interested* in it? Certainly; but what is
it to be interested in what you are doing? I suggest: to consider the
factors which determine what you do at any point an adequate
reason for doing it.

Stress is sometimes laid on Øing successfully, but a fair measure
of failure seems compatible with enjoyment. You can enjoy a game of
bridge at which you lose, or a day's fishing when you catch
nothing. A woman who looks after her baby attentively for the sake
of looking after it may not experience much pleasure if the child goes
from bad to worse and dies, but the explanation is not, I think, that
she is tending it unsuccessfully, but the bad health and impending
death of someone she loves keeps her in a predominantly anxious or
unhappy mood. A doctor might enjoy a brilliant but unsuccessful
fight for a patient's health. At any rate, when all these conditions are
fulfilled—when a person Øs voluntarily, attentively, for the sake of
Øing and with success, there is not just a psychological but a logical
presumption that his Øing is a pleasure; and if he says he has not
enjoyed himself, and cannot give us any reason why not, we may
refuse to accept his statement. As Mr A. Kenny observes, the report
of the inveterate angler: ' "The conditions were perfect, the fishing
was excellent, and I felt in very good trim, but I didn't enjoy it" is
quite unconvincing as it stands.'[11]

Here, then, is an account of pleasure in doing things, and one
which makes no appeal to personal awareness of sensations. We
ought, however, to consider what sensations are, and in what way
they can be pleasant.

By a sensation is generally meant today something like a pain,
ache, twinge or tickle. The eighteenth-century view was that these
are objects of awareness: we feel or perceive them with a sort of
internal sense. That can hardly be right. When we feel a tickle,
there is always some physical thing we feel, even if we cannot
identify it, which is tickling us, and the sensation of being tickled is
awareness of that. When you plunge your hand into boiling water,
what you are aware of is the water, and the awareness is painful or a
pain. Sensations, in short, are not so much objects as modes of
awareness; but what modes? For we would not reckon the awareness
of just anything a sensation in the sense we are investigating.

Whenever we perceive a thing, or perceive something about a thing, we are exercising one or more of the senses, and the exercise of a sense is perceiving (or, occasionally, failing to perceive) by what have been called objects proper to the sense. Colour is proper to sight, sound to hearing, odour to smell, flavour to taste, and to the sense of feeling or touch, perhaps whatever falls within the hot-cold or wet-dry spectrum. I mean that seeing a thing is perceiving it, and whatever we perceive about it, by its colour, hearing is perceiving by sound, and so on. Colour, sound, odour, temperature and the like may be said to constitute the *perceivability* of things. Colour renders things perceivable by sight or by eye, sound by hearing or by ear, temperature by feeling or by the organs of feeling, which I take to be any parts of the body, e.g. a hand, a toe, which we use when we want to tell by feeling how hot or large a thing is or how it is shaped.

Of our expressions for these objects proper to particular senses, some are definite and others indefinite, and the latter go in pairs. Definite expressions are 'red', 'turquoise', 'pitch of middle c', 'as soft as a whisper', 'rose-scented', 'orange-flavoured', 'silky', 'icy'; and these can properly be called expressions for perceptible qualities; Indefinite are 'pale', 'dark', 'bright', 'dim', 'loud', 'soft', 'high', 'low', 'sweet', 'sour', 'hot', 'cold', and these are not so much expressions for perceptible qualities as expressions applied to things on the ground that, in their perceptible qualities, they exceed or fall short of some norm. The norm may be one of at least three things. It may be the average. A sweet orange is perhaps one sweeter than average. Or it may be the best for the thing. When we say that a man is looking pale, we often mean that he falls short of that degree of colour which is most healthy. Or it may be the best for perceiving; let us concentrate on this last possibility.

Given that our sense organs are in a certain state, and given certain conditions of observation, a thing may have perceptible qualities by which we can easily tell what perceptible qualities it has, or which make it hard or impossible to tell this. The sun is too bright for us to tell by looking, from the earth, what colour or shape it is. A red hot poker is too hot for us to tell by feeling what shape or temperature it is. A lemon is too sour for us to tell by taste what flavour it is. A thing's sound may be too loud for us to tell by hearing, at a given distance, what sound it is making. A thing may also be so loud that we cannot tell what sound something else is making, but this is a different case which we shall consider later.

When a thing's colour, or sound, or temperature or the like is such that it is hard for a perceiver in a given situation to perceive it by the appropriate sense, then awareness of it by that sense is, I suggest, an unpleasant sensation. Awareness of the sun by sight, of boiling water by feeling, of an unsweetened lemon by taste, of excessively-loudsounding objects by hearing, are unpleasant sensations. We sufficiently understand what is meant by the unpleasantness of a sensation when we see how the situations I have described are unsatisfactory and how people try to avoid them—by ceasing to look or feel, trying to change the conditions of observation and the like.

It will be seen that the unpleasantness of a sensation depends on two factors, the perceptible qualities of the object and the situation of the perceiver, that is, the state of his sense organs, the conditions of observation and so on. The air around us is not in general unpleasant to feel, but when you have scalded your hand, feeling it is an unpleasant sensation. When either or both these factors are so changed that perception becomes easy again, awareness during the process or for a while afterwards may be a pleasant sensation. Thus when a shortsighted person puts on his spectacles and things come back into focus, or when you enter a concert hall after waiting outside for half a movement and can hear properly, seeing and hearing might be pleasant sensations. Similarly when we come into a warm room from the cold, or when we are parched after exertion on a hot day and drink a long draught of cool beer. These sensations may be called pleasant because of their contrast with the unpleasant sensations which precede or are mixed with them.[12]

But it may be thought that we sometimes have pleasant sensations which are not preceded by or mixed with pain, namely when we are aware of something which in its perceptible qualities is particularly well adapted to being perceived by us. Let us consider this in connection with sound.[13]

If a thing executes some thirty or more movements a second, it is audible. If it makes the same movement each time, or imparts the same sort of wave to the air, it has a pitch, and is said to make a sound in the strict sense; if its movement is irregular, it has no pitch and is said to make a noise. The more movements or vibrations a sounding body makes in a given time, the higher its pitch, and specific pitches like the pitch of middle c may be defined by the number of vibrations a second needed to produce them. When two things sound together, the waves they make in the air combine. If the number of movements made by the one in a given time stands to the number made by the other in a simple ratio like 1:2, 2:3, or 3:4 the wave pattern which results will be fairly even. In these cases the tones are said to be consonant or at consonant intervals of pitch. In other cases (the tones being at what are called dissonant intervals), the effect of the combination of the waves will be that a few waves are sensibly more intense than the rest, and the loudness of the sound will therefore be subject to sudden changes, making it hard for us to hear what the two pitches are. Most bodies which sound in fact produce a complex sound, made up of a fundamental tone or pitch, and a number of overtones at higher pitches. These overtones (which determine the timbre of the sounding body) may be at consonant or at dissonant intervals. If the hearing of what is well adapted for hearing is a pleasant sensation, we would expect things which make a sound to be pleasanter than things which make a noise (for since the latter have no pitch we cannot hear it), things sounding at consonant intervals to be pleasanter than things sounding at dissonant, and things with overtones at constant intervals to be pleasanter than things with overtones at dissonant. And that is what we do find. Musical instruments sound, and as objects of hearing are preferable to things like lorries which make a noise. Consonances are preferred to dissonances, and of musical instruments, those with consonant overtones like the piano, the violin, are preferred to those with dissonant, like the bell, the drum.

Much work on the physics of musical sound and the physiology of hearing was done by H. von Helmholtz, but Helmholtz was careful to keep natural science and aesthetics apart, and spoke of his researches as 'confined to the lowest grade of musical grammar'—accidence rather than syntax, let alone style.[14] What, in fact, have pleasant sensations to do with the pleasure given us by music? No simple and universal answer can be given, but perhaps we may say this. When a piece of music gives us pleasure, our pleasure consists primarily in hearing or listening to it, listening to it being an activity. In listening to a piece of music with pleasure we will have pleasant sensations, and these sensations may sometimes, and to some extent, make the listening a pleasure. If a piece of Bach or Schubert is played on a good piano, such as give us pleasant sensations, it will probably be easier and pleasanter to listen to it. And more significant, a composer may insert consonant chords and the like into a piece of music to refresh and gladden us. Although, however, pleasant sensations may thus render our listening enjoyable, there is a distinction between what enables us to enjoy something and what we are enabled to enjoy—Julia's confession that she loves you renders a normally dull walk enjoyable, but it is the walk, not her confession or love, which you enjoy—and when we listen to music, the object of our enjoyment is rather the piece of music itself, the change in sound, than the auditory sensations. Further, the pleasantness of listening seems to be logically prior to the pleasantness of the sensations. Even when the former results from the latter, I think the sensations are rather called pleasant because they cause or contribute to our pleasure in listening, than the listening pleasant because it results from pleasant sensations.

It may be added that unpleasant sensations, dissonances and the like, may also cause pleasure: they may keep our attention alive, and render hearing the consonances which follow them a pleasant sensation of relief—if, indeed, their unpleasantness is not exaggerated. Helmholtz argued that they are unpleasant on the ground that they irritate and reduce the efficiency of the inner ear: a good argument if what he says is true, but it is speculative. It might be that instead of favouring flutes and violins because they have overtones at consonant intervals, we favour consonant intervals because they are exhibited by these instruments.

What has been said about sensations of hearing may be applied to visual sensations. It may be that there are shades of colour which make seeing particularly easy, so that seeing them is a pleasant sensation, and we can find suggestions in some writers that being so coloured is in itself an aesthetic merit. One thing required for beauty, says Aquinas, 'is clarity; hence things which have a shining colour (*colorem nitidum*) are called beautiful'.[15] Clarity or 'shining-ness' would no doubt belong to stained glass like that at Chartres, and also to precious metals, 'gold' and 'silver' being reckoned names of colours. Plato perhaps credits Hippias with a similar idea when he makes him suggest that gold is the single thing, presence of in anything makes it beautiful.[16] In fact it seems that gold and shining colours can at most only assist or enable a beholder to take pleasure in contemplating a pattern.

4. *Following a piece of music*

We are considering the possibility that a piece of music is a success if listening to it is a pleasure. A variety of things extraneous to the piece may make listening to it a pleasure: the hearer may be in a mood to be pleased, the circumstances of the performance may be conducive to pleasure, and so forth; but we are looking for features in the piece itself which may lead us to expect that listeners will be pleased. To find them we must see more clearly what is involved in listening to music.

A piece of music is a change in sound, and we speak of following a process or change. I suggest that listening to music is trying to follow the change in sound, and that the music has merit by formalist criteria if it is a change which it is easy for people who are in general able to follow music, or music of that type, to follow attentively. What is it, then, to follow a change in sound?

Although we are mentally active when we follow a process, following it does not seem to be itself a specific kind of mental activity. In particular, though some turns in a process might have been predicted on the basis of what went before, following the process is not deducing what will happen next or even seeing that each development is deducible from its predecessors.[17] To say that a person is following a process is to attribute to him rather a state or capacity than an activity. On the other hand, though you can hardly be following a process if you remember nothing of what has happened the bare ability to remember what has happened is not enough: you may be able to recite every event in a sequence you found quite unfollowable.

It seems that anyone who is following any sort of process must know what is going on at any moment. Thus a person is following a game so long as he knows the state of the game; a spectator at cricket who cannot say which side is batting or what the score is or anything like that, however he may be straining his eyes, is not following the game. Similarly you are following events in Cambodia if you know what is happening in Cambodia; and (see below pp. 118-9) you are following a story if you know how things stand with the people in it.

This being so, a person following an instrument's change in sound must in the first place be able to tell, at any moment, how it is changing in sound, whether it is rising or falling in pitch or poised at the top, whether it is getting louder or softer or faster or slower, and, if the timbre changes, as in orchestral music, in what way it is changing. Changes of this sort are sometimes called slopes, and it is clearly basic to following and enjoying a piece of music to be aware of them, to know how it is 'sloping'.

Merely to know this, however, sounds hardly sufficient, so let us add as a second requirement that the listener should know where he is in the change at any moment. Obviously if we do not know where we are, if we have, so to speak, got lost in a piece of music, we can neither follow nor enjoy it; but what is it to know where you are? The change may be in any one or more of the three respects pitch, timbre and loudness, but let us for the sake of simplicity think of it as primarily one of pitch: what is said about changes in pitch may be applied to changes in loudness or timbre. To know where you are in a change of pitch is to be able to tell what the pitch is at any moment, not the absolute pitch, however, but the pitch relative to the pitch at other moments. You must be able to tell, in other words, at what intervals the notes are.

Formalists usually hold that a large part of aesthetic excellence is unity, but find it hard to explain wherein unity consists. What has just been said throws some light on this problem. If a piece of music is to succeed we must of course be able to distinguish it from changes in sound in the auditorium which precede and follow it, and it must also seem to be one piece, even though one with parts, and not an indeterminate number. If it is to seem one piece, the notes must seem to be related. Their relations can be relations only of pitch, timbre and loudness. So they will seem related if we can grasp their pitch intervals, if each is pitched so that we can hear the relative pitch of the others.

Musical notes succeed each other rapidly, and a great number of different sounds can be differentiated by the human ear; on the face of it, then, we might expect a hearer to have much difficulty in telling where he is; and some of the main features of music may be seen as devices to assist him.

The interval between two tones may be specified by the ratio of their vibrations. If there are two vibrations of one tone in the time of one vibration of the other, the tones are at the interval called an octave. If the ratio is three to two, the interval is a fifth, and the other intervals, third, fourth, sixth, etc., are similarly definable. The listener will clearly be helped if the composer uses only notes which are at definite, easily grasped intervals from one another. A system of intervals is what is called a scale, and music is in fact written in scales. Intervals of less than 15 : 16 are hard to detect, and are in fact avoided.[18] The interval which is easiest to grasp is the octave, probably not because the ratio 1 : 2 is easily grasped, but because the first consonant overtone of any tone is an octave above it, so that a listener hearing a tone and then its octave played on the piano hears something he already knows. Next comes the fifth, for similar reasons. In practice, all scales have these two intervals. Different societies have filled in slightly differently the other intervals, i.e. those between 2 : 3 and 15 : 16, but if the aim is to have as many tones as possible at intervals as easy as possible to grasp, a scale which approximates well to this ideal is the diatonic scale, and that is the scale which has in fact prevailed in Europe since classical Greek times.

While it is a help to the listener if all the notes in a piece he is trying to follow belong to a single scale, he has still to orientate himself, find where he is in the scale. The diatonic scale consists of alternating groups of two and three tone-intervals separated by semitones. Suppose, then, a note N is played: even if we know that the piece is in the diatonic scale, where in the scale is N? The intervals above it might go in any one of seven ways: tone, tone, semitone, tone, tone, tone, semitone; or tone, semitone, tone, tone, tone, semitone, tone; or semitone, tone, tone, tone, semitone, tone, tone; and so on. The usual practice of post-medieval composers has been to make clear to the listener one note, above which he may understand the scale to go in the first of the ways just indicated. This note determines and gives its name to the key. The composer then tends to restrict himself to the key he has settled for, though special effects can be achieved by departing from it, or, in a long piece of music, he may move into another key, usually one related to the first, for instance the key at the easily grasped interval of a fifth above. Ancient musicians seem to have adopted a different, but comparable practice: having directed attention to one note, they selected one of the seven modes of developing the scale above it, and stuck to that.[19] This is called composing in a mode, by contrast with composing in a key.

Scales, modes and keys were not evolved with the conscious intention of making pieces of music easy to follow, but it is hard to doubt that they caught on and became permanent features of music because that was their effect. Now it is fairly clear that a composer who scorns scales and keys and prescribes a series of absolute pitches, will have written a piece of music which it is impossible to follow; but in what way precisely does an ordinary listener tell the pitch of the notes in a straightforward piece written in the key of C major? For he cannot name each note as it is played, or state in words its interval from C.

In the first place, an ordinary piece of music does not consist of one long change in sound; rather, a short change or sequence only a few bars long is given out, and then repeated, varied, followed by something similar. As a result, the listener comes to know the sequence, and when a repetition or variation is played he can easily tell where he is in it. We may notice here that a piece of music may not please until we have heard it several times. People sometimes have this experience with elaborate plainsong graduals: at first the music is quite incomprehensible, and as they become familiar with it, pleasure in it increases.

Sometimes a piece can be followed at first hearing. It is plain evidence that a person has followed it, that he can hum or sing it:

he must then know the notes, even if he cannot name them. But even if he cannot reproduce the piece, we may say he knows what notes are being played if he is in a position to pronounce any note too high or low, too loud or soft, too long or short, or just right. A note is too high or low, loud or soft, in this context, if it diverges not from what is best for hearing it, but from what is best for hearing the other notes. It detains us while we try to place it, so that we have to race to catch up, it introduces an ambiguity into what is happening, it has itself a misleading prominence or it deprives other notes of the prominence they require. If there can be an ambiguity the music must in general be clear, and if we can be misled, we must be being led or following. It is the mark of the inexperienced gradual-hearer's inability to follow the music, that he cannot tell whether notes are right or wrong.

Again, and perhaps most important, a piece of music is often said to contain tensions, surprises and the like; that is, it arouses expectations, delays their satisfaction, or disappoints them. At an elementary level, if the music gets higher or louder we expect the change to come to an end and be reversed. More subtle, we listen for particular sequences of notes and even for single notes—an obvious example is the key-note at the end. Clearly having such expectations is an essential part of following a piece of music; but what is the nature of them? Professor G. Ryle suggested that when a gardener expects rain his expectation consists not in verbal presages, but in keeping his coat by him, bedding out seedlings and the like.[20] The ordinary listener to music does not and often could not formulate his expectations under his breath, but what is the coat he keeps by him? When the music is getting higher and we expect it to get lower, this, I suggest, is simply part of our understanding that it is getting higher. Compare our expectation that it will become dark, which is not something additional to, but rather part of, our understanding that dusk is falling. And similarly when we listen for a particular note or sequence of notes, that is not something apart from listening to the notes being played at the moment: it is not a distraction from them, rendering us inattentive to them, as listening for a train may make us inattentive to what a companion is saying, but rather a mode of attention to them. But what mode? It is hearing them as related to others in pitch, loudness etc.

If the pleasure of listening to music is to be like other pleasures, in listening to music we must do things in a manner determined by factors internal to the activity. Part, at least, of what we are doing is listening for developments; and what we listen for at any moment is determined by what we have heard already. I said that a person could enjoy a game of bridge even if he made the wrong plays, so long as what plays he made were determined by factors internal to the game. In the same way it is not impossible that two people should hear a piece of music differently, and both get pleasure from it; and perhaps there is no single best way of hearing some pieces, as there is hardly a best way of playing some hands at Bridge.

When we enjoy an activity, not only is what we do determined by factors internal to the activity, but those factors seem by themselves a sufficient reason for doing it. If listening to a piece of music is to stand a good chance of satisfying this requirement, the piece must contain variety, surprises, even some difficulty. Suppose a piece of music consisted of a note and the fifth above played a hundred times: the interval would be easy to grasp; but the sounding of the lower note would soon cease to be an adequate reason for listening for the higher, and only politeness or the like would keep a hearer attentive. As a bridge player may enjoy a difficult hand more than an easy one, and would certainly not enjoy playing the same hand over and over all evening, so the hearer must be kept interested; and while it would be absurd to lay down rules for sustaining interest, critics can and do point to features in particular pieces which may reasonably be expected to have that effect. And in general, we might say, if a piece is to be interesting, if a hearer is to listen constantly in the appropriate way because of what has gone before, the piece must be such that the hearer cannot afford to miss many notes without getting lost.

Enough has perhaps now been said to indicate how a piece of music can succeed by formalist criteria. We should recognise, of course, that such criteria are not always the most appropriate. Some music is intended to represent; and music is sometimes valued because of some connection it has with feelings and emotions. I shall come to these topics later, but before we leave the pleasures of following a change in sound, a further word may be added.

Although following a process is not deducing what turns it will take, and is compatible with being surprised, surprising turns ought to be understandable: sooner or later we should be able to find something which will explain them. Suppose you are watching a game of bridge and you see the declarer early in the hand give up a trick which it seems he did not have to lose, at least at that juncture; this may at first surprise you, but then you realise that he is rectifying the count in preparation for a squeeze. Your puzzlement is removed by a description of what is happening which is fairly profound and

technical. In the same way[21] a sophisticated hearer can supply fairly
technical descriptions of what is happening in a piece of music:
it has changed from G major to G minor, the former tune is being
inverted, or the like. In the light of such descriptions, surprising
notes and developments can be seen, not as inevitable, but as
desirable; we can recognise that a discord or apparently random
note has after all a relation to the rest. The fuller and deeper descriptions a hearer can supply, the better he follows the music, and,
we may suppose, if he follows it without effort, the more he enjoys it.

5. *Following a pattern*

Can a similar account be given of patterns? A pattern is a variation
in visible qualities, such as colour, size, shape, extending through
space. Pictures, representational as well as abstract, and also woods
in spring, mountain landscapes, sunsets and the like, exemplify
variations in colour; and it is possible that when they please it is
because the variations are easy to follow, because we can easily tell
the colour at various points, and the colours at different points
bring one another out, render one another visible. That colours can
affect one another, that the same expanse can look different in
colour (and also size and shape) when juxtaposed to different colours,
has been established by many psychological experiments.[22]

But although it is a plausible surmise that some patterns succeed
because the variations in colour are a pleasure to follow, it seems
impossible, in our present state of scientific knowledge[23], to offer any
objective criteria of success. In music there are recognised pitches,
timbres, intervals and the like, which can be given precise physical
definitions. There are no recognised colour intervals, and the colour
words in ordinary use like 'red', 'blue' are not associated with any
definite light-frequencies or ranges of light-frequencies. (Newton's
division of the spectrum into seven colours was not based on considerations of light or colour, but simply an attempt to provide an
analogue to the notes of the scale.) A little experimental work has
been done on the aesthetic effect of colour combinations, but the
findings are too crude to provide a basis for judging ordinary works
of art.[24] There is no satisfactory way even of describing a given colour
sample. People usually distinguish three coordinates, so to speak, of
colour: hue, in respect of which green differs from red; brightness,
in respect of which white differs from black; and saturation, in
respect of which a pure green like that in the spectrum differs from a
greyish green like that of the North Sea. It is not natural to class in
any of these ways the important difference between a colour thinned

with turpentine and the same colour thinned with linseed oil. Bright and dim are different from pale and dark, and shining and dull are different again. Traditional heraldry divides colour-expressions into expressions for tinctures, metals and furs; modern writers deal only with tincture-colours; but just why we should set aside metals and furs, and say that lemon, orange and vermilion are colours but gold, copper and fox are not, is unclear.

About variations in size and shape we can speak more precisely; but first, is there any need? Although Bell and Mrs Langer, as we saw, do not in the end offer strictly formalist criteria, other writers do, and without requiring us to consider what it is to follow a change.

Instead, they tend to appeal to gestalt psychology. Gestalt psychologists hold[25] that the primary data of experience are not (as Hume and Kant thought) raw sensations, but 'structures', *Gestalten*, which already have a certain complexity and organisation, like geometrical shapes, or variations or equalities in colour or feel. A 'step up' in brightness from one patch to another would be a structure. A structure may be strong, stable and clear, in which case it holds steady before our awareness, or it may be weak and obscure, in which case it gives the illusion (if 'illusion' is the right word) of wavering before us, and we involuntarily endeavour to strengthen it in various ways: for instance if two areas differ slightly in colour, we tend either to see them as the same colour, or to exaggerate the difference until we have a clear colour 'step'; if there are small bits missing from the circumference of a circle we tend to fill them in. It is easy to understand that such a theory was read with avidity by aestheticians, and that some simply identified being an aesthetically good pattern with being a strong *Gestalt*.[26] Certainly if strong *Gestalten* are what in general we strive to see, we may suppose that when something is strong *Gestalt*, contemplating it will be pleasant. However, the gestalt psychologists' explanation of what makes a structure strong—or, if a strong structure is defined as one we tend to see, then why we tend to see some patterns rather than others, may deter us from leaning on the theory with all our weight.

Mr R. Arnheim's account of balance in patterns will illustrate what I mean.[27] He begins by pointing out that a pattern consisting of a square and a relatively small circle will be balanced if the circle is in the middle of the square; otherwise the pattern will be unbalanced, and the circle will have a tendency to move about, unless it is counterbalanced by another circle placed symmetrically opposite. Proceeding to more complex examples (and he can use as an illustration a design by Ben Nicholson), Arnheim suggests that we may test a

pattern for balance by allotting weight to the elements in it in proportion to their size and calculating whether, at the distances at
which they are, they compensate about the centre like real weights
about a fulcrum: it is possible to trace perceptual forces in a pattern
analogous to the mechanical forces in a mechanical structure.

Arnheim is, I think, right that whether a pattern has balance can
be demonstrated, at least up to a point, in this way; but talk about
perceptual forces needs interpretation, since the perceptual centres
of force, the centre of the pattern, the corners and so on, do not exert
on elements in the pattern forces recognised by ordinary science; and
Arnheim favours the following interpretation, which is taken from
gestalt psychology. At the back of the brain there exists a field of
electro-chemical forces. When a pattern stimulates the eye, activity
occurs in this region, and a pattern of real electrical forces is produced
which mirrors, or perhaps we should say is 'topologically similar'
to the pattern seen. If the electrical forces in the brain are in equili-
brium and the pattern there is stable, our awareness is steady
awareness of a strong *Gestalt*, and we call the visible pattern balanced;
if the visible pattern is unbalanced and the elements move about,
their apparent movement is due to erratic electrical activity in the
brain.

The chief trouble with this account is not that it is a tissue of
conjectures, but that Arnheim has fallen into an error typical, as its
critics have pointed out,[25] of gestalt psychology, and assimilated contemplating a pattern to having a sensation. We saw that we have a
sensation when the exercise of a sense is physically impeded or
facilitated. On Arnheim's showing, an unbalanced pattern is one
which physically impedes vision, by causing an unstable brain state,
and a balanced pattern one which physically aids vision, causing a
brain state which enables us to contemplate the pattern steadily.
A balanced pattern, then, is one which gives us a pleasant sensation.
This is an error, because whether a pattern has balance is something
we asertain by exercising the sense of sight. In ascertaining it we
might have visual sensations, for instance if the pattern is so close to
the eye that rays from it do not focus at the right place behind the
optic lens, so that we have a sensation of blurred vision. But there
must always be a difference between any question we are trying to
answer and the question whether our attempt to answer it is being
aided or impeded. If this holds generally for features constituting
aesthetic merit, that we try to perceive whether things have them,
aesthetic merit cannot be an aptitude to give pleasant sensations, and
it is inappropiate to offer a physiological account of it.

Mr H. Osborne holds that a pattern has aesthetic merit (and similarly anything else, for he allows only one criterion of aesthetic assessment), if and only if it has a certain configurational unity, a certain organic wholeness inviting us to perceive it as a whole, which he nevertheless wishes to distinguish from the unity of a strong *Gestalt*.[28] His main reason is not the one given above, but that gestalt theory requires us to perceive figures against grounds while in aesthetic contemplation, he claims, ground and figure are not distinguished. The weakness of his theory, as critics of his book *Theory of beauty* have emphasised,[29] is that it is then unclear what this important kind of unity is: he will find it hard to deny it to anything which we perceive and are aware of as a physical object of some definite sort.

Although Arnheim plumps for a wrong account, he makes remarks which point to a better. It is true that we cannot keep an unbalanced element, say a circle randomly situated in a square, in its place. The reason is that we do not know its place. The centres of perceptual force or attraction, like the centre and corners of a square, are the places which can most easily be seen and identified, and that constitutes their attraction. Again, Arnheim describes bad features of a design as 'ambiguous' and 'equivocal', expressions which apply to things as objects of thought, not as causes of brain states, and he says of an unsatisfactory pattern: 'Proportions are based on small differences, which leave the eye uncertain whether it deals with equality or inequality, square or rectangle. We cannot tell what the pattern is trying to say.' This suggests that if a pattern is to be a success it must be clear, not only where the elements are, but whether they are the same or different in size and what shape they are. And that is to say that the pattern must be followable. If to follow a piece of music is to be able to tell the pitch, loudness etc. of the notes, to follow a pattern is to be able to tell the place, size, shape etc. of the elements.

We may reach the same position by a slightly different route. If a pattern is to have unity, it must be clear that the elements in it are related. Some ambitious Victorian buildings lack unity and fail aesthetically because the parts—towers, windows, projections and so on—seem unrelated. Now what are the elements of a pattern? If we set aside colours there remain lines, areas, volumes, angles, curves, and the shapes these make up. We may count among elements in a pattern not only the lines and areas actually marked but also such divisions of these as it is natural to see; for instance it is natural to see in a rectangle with sides 2 : 1 the squares which are its halves. How can such elements be related? There is only one way possible: quantitatively. A distance, area or angle may be equal to, or some multiple or fraction of, another. So it is relations of this sort which must be clear. A pattern has unity insofar as the beholder can tell how great each distance, angle etc. is, not absolutely, but in relation to the others. That is, once again, the pattern must be followable.

The suggestion that a pattern is a success if it is easy and pleasant to follow, and a failure if the beholder gets lost in it, may be worked out in the same way as the corresponding suggestion about music. We can show that if a pattern satisfies certain conditions it will be possible or easy to follow; we can say that the beholder knows where he is, or what particular elements are in relation to others, if he can pronounce elements too large, too small or just right; and we can show by examples the importance of variety, surprise, and even difficulty in sustaining interest so that the following is pleasurable. I shall here develop only the first point; it if is indeed true that there are features which make a pattern followable, and if patterns which are considered aesthetically good have such features, that is some support for our suggestion.

Consider that simple and ubiquitous pattern the logarithmic spiral. A logarithmic spiral may be constructed in various ways, but the following crude method will suffice.

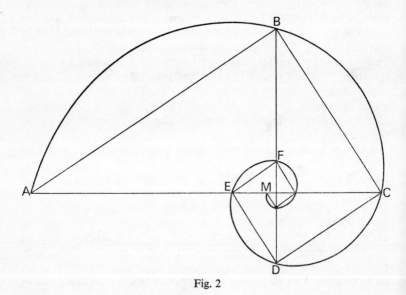

Fig. 2

Take any right-angled triangle ABC (only let it not be isosceles, or you obtain a circle), and drop a perpendicular from B to AC, cutting AC at M, and cutting a line drawn from C at right angles to BC at D. A line drawn at right angles to CD from D cuts AM at E; a line similarly drawn from E cuts BM at F. Continue drawing such lines, and you obtain a rectangular spiral; and AM, BM, CM, DM etc., are vectors of a curved logarithmic spiral. Patterns approximating to these two spirals are used in decoration in all ages and places, and are easy to follow. The curved spiral has unity and continuity, because it is curving at a constant angle: a tangent to any vector makes the same angle. And the vectors change in length in a regular way: as AM is to BM, so BM is to CM, and as BM to CM, so CM to DM. The lines composing the rectangular spiral are also in continued proportion; and the successive triangles ABC, BCD, CDE etc. are the same shape, and vary in size in a constant manner which may, if suitable values are chosen, be easily grasped. If AB : BC :: n : 1, ABC : BCD :: n^2 : 1. Hence if AB : BC :: $\sqrt{2}$: 1, ABC : BCD :: 2 : 1, a very easily grasped relationship.

This last point prepares us for what might otherwise have been surprising. If the aim is to have elements the relationship of which is easily grasped, we might expect designers to avoid incommensurable lines, lines which stand in such ratios as $\sqrt{2}$: 1, $\sqrt{5}$: 1. In fact, they favour them; and we can see that they have the advantage that with them we may construct figures with easily commensurable areas. If a rectangle has sides in the ratio $\sqrt{2}$: 1, it can be divided into two halves which are the same shape, $\sqrt{2}$: 1. A square has not this property, and a beholder can thus more easily take in the halves of the $\sqrt{2}$ rectangle than the halves of the square.

A spiral, in which the various parts are related in a steady, simple way, may be compared with a scale in music, and has perhaps the same modest claim to be called a pattern which a scale has to be called a piece of music. The parallel can be extended. We have modes and keys, and the key of C major, or the Greek Lydian mode, has a sort of primacy in music. In the same way we have qualitatively different spirals as the angle or curvature or the ratio of successive sides varies; and a ratio central to visual design seems to be that of $\sqrt{5}-1$: 2. This is the so-called Golden Section, and the ratio to which successive terms of the Fibonacci series 0, 1, 1, 2, 3, 5, 8, 13 . . . approximate. Rectangular and curved spirals based on it are generally considered highly satisfactory.

If spirals are comparable to modes or keys, we might hope to find that more complex patterns are composed out of the elements we discovered in spirals, and an attempt to show this for Greek temples and vases was in fact made by Jay Hambridge in *Dynamic symmetry: the Greek vase* and *The Parthenon and other Greek temples: their dynamic symmetry*.[30] It is difficult for a reader to assess Hambridge's results. On the one hand, the operation calls for accurate measurement which cannot be checked from photographs; on the other, to break down a complicated pattern into elements calls for ingenuity a little like that exercised in finding cryptograms in Shakespeare. Hambridge can, however, produce some evidence that ancient artists actually used the constructions necessary for designs with elements commensurable only in area or square, and we have, I think, some grounds for saying, both that ancient patterns are, and that they are intended to be, successful by the criterion of being easy and pleasant to follow.

Even if these principles of design were followed consciously only by the Greeks and, perhaps, the Egyptians, other nations could have used them unconsciously. Indeed, just as we find nations who knew nothing of the ratios determining the diatonic scale, still using parts of it, so wherever design is taken seriously we would expect to find spirals and proportions approximating to the mathematical norms; and in fact that is what we do find.

Living things in general grow in a logarithmic manner; nature produces many spirals, for instance in shells and horns; the leaves of plants, when exposure to light and air is beneficial, grow in a spiral, the angle between each two approximating to the inverse angle of $\dfrac{\sqrt{5}-1}{2}$ of 360°; and when leaves or seeds form a pattern of spirals unwinding in opposite directions, as happens with a sunflower head, the numbers of the spirals in the two directions tend to be successive terms of the Fibonacci series.[31] For these reasons it has been thought that spiral patterns are expressive or symbolic of life and growth, and that therein lies their aesthetic value.[32] If, however, a pattern is to please because it is a pattern in which things grow, we must know that things grow in that pattern; and it seems that we can be pleased by spirals while knowing nothing of phyllotaxis or molecular growth. If that is so, we are rather pleased by shells because they are spirals than by spirals because they are like shells; and we are pleased by spirals because they are easy to follow.

Aestheticians who advocate formalist criteria often contrast 'discursive' with 'synoptic' perception, going over and connecting up the parts of an object of awareness with contemplating it as a whole; and they say that the former is characteristic of scientific observation and practical life, while the latter is typically aesthetic.[33] Insofar as the distinction is valid, in this chapter I have urged just the opposite. Contemplating a pattern synoptically or all at once would be contemplating it as the end of a temporal process, and if we are to enjoy it we must rather contemplate it discursively as a spatial process. It would be more 'aesthetic' to contemplate a triangle as the passing away of the base-line in the height than as a static shape. But in fact the distinction is not too clear. On the one hand, even if the scientist or practical man is to observe some part of what is before him, he must be aware of it as some sort of unified whole or at least through awareness of such a whole. If I attend to a nose, a nose is from a logical point of view a unified physical object, a thing falling under a sortal concept; if I attend to a square inch of your skin, I identify this square inch as the square inch half way down your neck, and your neck, to say nothing of you, is a unity and a whole. On the other hand, aestheticians who favour synoptic (and, I suppose, synacoustic) perception, are not very explicit about what it is; they usually advise us to learn by introspection: if a down-to-earth account could be given of what they have in mind, it might turn out to be pretty similar to what I call following a change in respect of perceptible qualities.[34]

3

REPRESENTATION

1. *What is a representation?*

Many works of art are representations. Picture galleries containing pictures painted before 1900 are full of them. Plays and works of literature also seem to be representations of a sort; at least we talk about the way in which a novelist or dramatist has depicted a person or situation. And there is a representative element in some musical compositions, in operatic storm music, melodies written to fit the words of songs, and so on.

Some aestheticians hold that even when a work of art is a representation, it is not as a representation that we view it when we assess it aesthetically. It has been claimed, for instance, that a portrait has aesthetic merit only if the pattern on the canvas is superior to that exemplified by the sitter's face.[1] Now it is certainly possible to judge a portrait by this criterion, but it is not at all clear why this should be the only aesthetic way of judging it; and when we have to do with a painstaking experimenter in representational effects like Leonardo or Constable,[2] it is the extreme of perversity to assess his works simply as abstract patterns. The making light of representation as such is quite a modern and localised phenomenon. If we consider the critical approach, not just of the twentieth-century West, but of other ages and societies, we find that mimetic criteria, criteria by which things are assessed aesthetically as representations, have been far more popular than any others. Indeed, many aestheticians, neo-platonic, medieval and oriental, have treated not only pictures and poems, but works of pottery and carpentry as representations: the craftsman, they have said,[3] is representing an ideal artefact which he sees by intellectual intuition. This particular idea, I shall argue, rests on a mistake; but in general the importance of mimetic criteria cannot seriously be denied, and we must see what they are, how they work, and whether they can be adapted to things which are not representations.

First, what exactly is a representation?—for, as I indicated in Chapter 1, the notion of representation is difficult. I shall confine myself here to pictorial representation, because pictures are the clearest examples of representations; how far it is correct to call works of literature representations and apply mimetic criteria to them will be discussed in Chapter 5.

It is sometimes suggested that representation can be explained in terms of seeing as;[4] but this suggestion will not, I think, stand up. We talk of seeing as when we have an object of vision which may be interpreted in various ways, as satisfying more concepts than one. Wittgenstein discusses seeing as in *Philosophical investigations*, II, xi and gives, among other examples, the drawing:

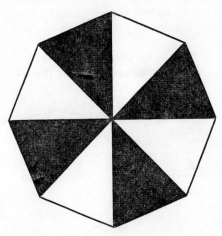

Fig. 3

This, he observes, can be seen either as a black cross on a white background, or as a white cross on a black background. In general to see something is to be aware of it by the sense of sight (it is not a sufficient condition of your having seen something, that it has affected your retina: consider playing hunt the thimble); and we can be aware of something only under some description, however vague, only as something falling under some concept. If, however, it is obvious that something satisfies a particular concept, we do not say we see it as

satisfying that concept. I do not say when I sit down to lunch: 'I
see this as a plate'. We say that an object was seen as something f,
when it really is, or might more naturally have been thought of as,
something else g. The bush detective saw the motionless aborigine as
a dead tree stump; the artist saw the child's face as a pattern of
smudgy shadows.

If representation is to be explained in terms of seeing as, it must
be in the following simple way. A painted canvas may be seen as a
painted canvas, but it may also be seen as something else, e.g. a
bowl of fruit or a seated lady; and it is called a representation of a
bowl of fruit or seated lady for just that reason, because a bowl
of fruit or seated lady is something it can be seen as. The weakness
of this explanation is obvious. It reduces representation to illusion,
and all pictures to attempts at *trompe l'oeil* painting.[5] If there is a
trompe l'oeil picture of a letter-rack on the wall, I may see it as a
letter rack. But in the way in which I see the *trompe l'oeil* picture as a
letter rack, I certainly do not see a picture by Cezanne of Mt Ste
Victoire as Mt Ste Victoire. At the best I see it as a picture of Mt Ste
Victoire.

Wittgenstein is perhaps to blame if the difference is sometimes
overlooked. In his discussion of seeing as he presents the drawing:

Fig. 4

and says: 'It can be seen as a rabbit's head or as a duck's'. What he
should have said is: 'It can be seen as a drawing of a rabbit's head
or as a drawing of a duck's'. In general, it is true enough that any
representative picture can be seen either as a coloured surface or as a

representation of something; but to say this is not to explain representation in terms of seeing as: a representation is something as which something can be seen.

Even if we could explain representing as enabling the beholder to see as, the explanation would not take us very far. We want to talk about objects in pictures, about the face, say, in a Rembrandt picture of an old woman. Are we to say we are talking about the face we see this part of the canvas as? What then is the status of a face something is seen as? How does it compare with other faces? Where is it? I hope not in somebody's mind, that favourite bolt-hole of doubtful entities when the philosopher heaves in sight.

Instead of seeking a short cut by way of seeing as, let us start from the beginning and see what can be said of a typical representation, say a naturalistic picture of a horse painted in oils on canvas. And first, of what is it that we say: 'That is a picture of a horse'? The most obvious answer is: of a certain coloured object. When I say: 'I have a picture of a horse in the back of my car' or 'A picture of a horse was destroyed in the fire' you understand me to be speaking of a coloured object.

What is the coloured object? If the question is what has been coloured, the natural answer is: a piece of canvas. Since, however, the artist coloured the canvas by smearing it with paint, we could say also that the coloured object is a piece of canvas with paint on it. (You can, of course, colour a thing without smearing anything on it, as when you project your photographic slides onto a screen.) Similarly the sort of thing of which we might say: 'That is a statue of a horse' is a piece of carved marble. And in the way in which the picture of the horse is a piece of canvas coloured in a certain way, a fresco is an expanse of plaster coloured in a certain way. Frescoes have lately become quite mobile, and it no longer surprises people if you say: 'I have a wall painting of the Last Supper in my van.'

The question 'What is a picture of a horse?' can be taken, and answered, in various ways, and one sort of answer has now been given: a picture of a horse is a coloured object. Compare showing someone round your collection of curiosities. 'That is a Caucasian distaff.' '*What* is a Caucasian distaff?' 'That piece of wood beside the wampum beads.' But the question may also be construed: what is it for a thing to be a picture of a horse? What makes a coloured object a picture of a horse? To this we may reply: the way it is coloured. A piece of canvas is a picture of a horse because a certain pattern extends over it, because various colours spread across it for distances in shapes.

Now if I analyse or specify the pattern which extends over the canvas, I give one sort of account of a picture of a horse. Two points about this account. First, although it is descriptive in a way it is also, in the sense indicated above p. 29 *prescriptive*: I am giving a prescription or formula for a picture of a horse, the prescription, in fact, which the artist followed. Second, there is no one prescription which an artist must follow if he is to make a piece of canvas into a picture of a horse. I do not mean that he will follow one formula if he is painting a drinking horse and another if he is painting a galloping horse, but two artists may both set out to depict the king on horseback taking the salute at a particular parade, and both may succeed, yet they may have coloured their canvasses very differently.

Obviously this is not the only sort of account I can give of a picture of a horse. I may say: 'It is a picture of a chestnut mare. She is grazing in a field, probably, because of the flowers and colour of the grass, in July. Behind her at the end of the field is a line of well-grown elms.' In short, I may say what is depicted, or represented, or simply happening, in the picture. And if the former account, in terms of colours extending for distances in shapes, was prescriptive, this account is descriptive: it is a description of a picture of a horse, of the picture produced by imparting the pattern to the canvas.

It is important to have the relation between these accounts clear. Both when I say 'Brown extends in an oblong left of centre' and when I say 'That animal is a horse; there are trees behind it', I am desscribing. But I am not describing quite the same thing in the two cases. It is natural to say that in the first case I am describing a piece of canvas, and in the second a picture. But neither am I describing two different things, for the canvas is the picture: they are not separate entities on all fours with one another like the text and the illustrations in a book. The position is that the canvas, being coloured as it is, *constitutes* a picture; and if I want to describe the picture in the sense of that which is constituted, to describe it by itself apart from what constitutes it, I must say what is represented, what it is a picture of.

What do I mean here by 'constitutes'? A great many things can be conceived and described in two ways. We might say that a pen-nib is a small, thin piece of hard stuff, longer than it is wide, tapered at one end, split at the taper end, and curved longitudinally into a half-cylinder. Or we might say that a pen-nib is an instrument for writing in ink. Although we are here giving two different accounts, we are not describing two different things. Rather, we would say that a thin piece of metal, shaped as has been said, constitutes an instrument for writing in ink. Again, though the example is perhaps more controversial, we can describe the physical structure of a dog, the arrangement of bones, sinews, entrails and so on; or we can say what a dog characteristically does, how dogs chase rabbits, and are kept in houses as guards and companions. A formation of flesh and bones is not something different from a retriever or watch-dog, but flesh and bones in this formation constitute such a thing. Adopting terminology which seems to be coming back into fashion,[6] we might say that the one description applies to the material aspect of a thing, and the other to the formal. So when we say how the canvas is coloured we describe the material aspect of a picture, and when we say what is represented or going on in it, the formal.[7]

Flesh and bone in a certain configuration constitute a horse; canvas coloured a certain way constitutes a picture or representation of a horse. This suggests that a representation is something logically analogous to what we might call a reality or real instance of something;[8] and that, in fact, seems to be the best way of understanding the notion of representation.

Our concept of a representation or picture is not on the same level as our concept of a chair or dog. Some ways of speaking obscure this. We might say: 'The attic contained a rug, a picture and a gigantic spider.' But this is really as odd as saying: 'The attic contained a picture of a rug, a real object, and a picture of a gigantic spider.' The world does not contain rugs, spiders and pictures; it contains rugs, spiders, pictures of rugs, toy spiders and the like; or else it contains real things, pictures, toys, forgeries, instruments etc. That is why I have been discussing, not just a picture, but a picture of a horse: it is fairly easy to give an account of a picture of a horse, as it is to give an account of a real horse; it is tricky to say what a picture is, as it is tricky to say what a real thing is.

I am suggesting that words like 'representation', 'represented' play the same sort of role in our speech as words like 'reality', 'real'. Thus the expression 'in a picture' functions like the expression 'in real life'. We can say that a horse is grazing in a field in a picture, as we can say that a horse is grazing in a field in real life. In the one case the horse is represented as grazing, in the other it really is grazing. A picture, however, is analogous, not so much to reality in general, as to an instant in reality. As a horse may be grazing at one instant and drinking at another, so it may be grazing in one picture and drinking in another. And as a horse cannot be in different places at the same instant, so it cannot be in different places in the same picture; if it seems to be, we must say, either that we have two horses of the same appearance, or else that we have two pictures run together, as in the Bayeux Tapestry.

Similarly the properties we assign to things in pictures are properties which (we claim at least) they are represented as having. If we say 'That animal is a horse' we mean that it is represented as being a horse, i.e. as having the nature, physical structure, dispositions to behave etc., of a horse. When we say 'The horse is in a field' we mean that it is represented as being in a field. Things in pictures are represented *instead of* existing, and the place of a represented thing is where it is represented as being. The material which constitutes Michelangelo's statue of Moses is in Rome; but Moses in Michelangelo's Moses is not in Rome (still less in anyone's mind) but in the vicinity of Mt Sinai.

Philosophical perplexity about things in pictures has mostly centred round their spatial properties and location. Mrs Langer writes about space in pictures: 'This purely visual space is an illusion, for our sensory experiences do not agree on it in their report. . . . Being only visual, this space has no continuity with space in which we live; it is limited by the frame, or by surrounding blanks, or incongruous other things which cut it off. Yet its limits cannot even be said to *divide* it from practical space; for a boundary that divides things always connects them as well, and between the picture space and any other space there is no connection. The created virtual space is entirely self-contained and independent.'[9]

Mrs Langer writes in a slightly prophetic style which excites misgivings among more academic thinkers, and Mr E. Bedford has recently argued that visual space cannot enjoy the logical independence she attributes to it.[10] Things in pictures, he claims, must stand in some spatial relations to things in real life. For in order to understand a picture at all, in order to see it as a picture and make out things in it, we must make certain primary identifications which concern patches of paint in the real world. 'What I identify as (not of course, with) *a cross* in Verrochio's painting, is a long thin area of paint at the right hand side.' So (we are apparently to conclude) the location of the cross in the picture is not logically independent of the location of physical objects in reality. This argument, however, seems to be defective.[11] The long thin area of paint is identified, not as a cross, but as a representation of a cross; and the represented cross is not at the right hand side of the picture, but somewhere in Palestine. Mrs Langer is, I think, right that 'visual space' is discontinuous with real space. It is the space things are represented as being in, and is a represented space. If we wish to criticise her account there are two other points on which we would do better to fasten.

First, represented space is not an illusion. It is not an illusion because we are not deceived: we do not think that a horse really is grazing in a field, but that a horse is represented as grazing in a field. She claims it as an illusion on the ground that senses other than sight, e.g. touch, will not confirm that things are at the distances from one another they appear to be. If we were looking at a *trompe l'oeil* picture we really might suffer an illusion, and detect it by our sense of touch; but in the case of an ordinary picture, what is important is not our sense of touch but the sense of touch of persons in the picture. Suppose we have a picture of a man taken in by a *trompe l'oeil* picture: we might say that the spatial relations of the things in the *trompe l'oeil* picture are illusory, as he would discover if he exercised his sense of touch.

Second, there is no good reason for saying that represented space is limited by the frame of the picture, and indeed to say that is to play into Bedford's hands. If a thing is represented as being in a spatial universe which is boundless, as I suppose most things are, the represented space is boundless. And we often know what is going on in parts of the represented space which do not appear in the picture. Take a picture of a king trembling on his throne at the news that his army has been wiped out: the picture shows us only the throne room, but we misunderstand it unless we realise that miles away there is a corpse-strewn battle field. Sometimes only the head and arms of a figure appear in the picture; yet we may still know the position of his legs, and do not think it is a picture of a man without a lower half.

What holds for spaces in pictures holds for spaces in novels. The London of Mr Dombey is in no spatial relations with the London of Queen Victoria, nor can Mr Dombey, when opening his *Times*, hope to read an article by Tom Towers.

So much on the places and spatial relations of things in pictures; something should also be said about their identity and individuality. In the first place, a picture is of individuals, such as Socrates, or Pegasus. That is, what is represented in a picture is an individual, whether real or fictitious, and whether named or nameless. Suppose I paint a picture of a horse and you ask 'What horse is that?' and I reply 'No particular horse; just a horse': it is still an individual horse. That is, 'a horse' in 'A horse is represented in that picture' is like 'a horse' in 'A horse kicked him' and not like 'A horse was a necessity for a doctor here once'. And it is the same if we say: 'A centaur is represented in that picture.'

It may be though that this involves a difficulty. For one way of explaining the difference between 'a horse' in 'A horse kicked him' and 'a horse' in 'A horse was a necessity for a country doctor' is this: we can say 'There was a horse that kicked him', but not 'There was a horse which was a necessity for a country doctor'—for there was no one horse that all the country doctors needed. Now if 'a centaur' in 'A centaur is kissing a nymph in that picture' is like 'a horse' in 'A horse kicked him', will we not have to say 'There is a centaur which is kissing (or is represented as kissing) a nymph'? No: we need say only 'There is represented in that picture a centaur which is kissing a nymph'. Representation is analogous to real existence, and we could speak if we like of representational quantification instead of existential quantification.

Individuals, then, are represented; and the converse of this is that nothing is represented as an individual. If I say, describing a picture, 'Socrates is sitting in prison' I mean that Socrates is represented as sitting in prison. But if I say 'The man on the bed is Socrates' I do not mean that the man on the bed is represented as Socrates. In a description of a picture we can replace 'is' by 'is represented as' only when it is used to predicate, as in 'Socrates is snubnosed', not when it is used to assert an identity, as here. An artist can represent any individual he pleases; which individual is represented in a picture depends on his intention—a matter which will be discussed below. And he can make his intention to represent Socrates clear, by representing Socrates as having the characteristics traditionally associated with him. But in the way he can represent the subject of his picture as snubnosed, he cannot represent him as a particular real or fictitious person. If he could, it could be part of what a picture showed, that what it showed was real or imaginary— which is obvious nonsense.

I said that in a description of a picture, an 'is' asserting an identity cannot be paraphrased as 'is represented as'. There is one rather complex exception. We believe that the John who really baptised Christ was the same man as the John who really denounced Herod for incest. What our grounds are for this belief does not matter so long as we have some. Perhaps companions of the Baptist kept him in view continuously and saw him denounce Herod. Now suppose an artist sees a picture of John baptising Christ; he may go off and paint a picture of John denouncing Herod, in which he represents John as the man who baptised Christ in the first picture, i.e. as satisfying criteria of personal identity with the man in that picture. Perhaps he represents him as similar in appearance and accompanied by similar disciples. In this case we may say that John in the second picture is, i.e. is intended to be, the same man as the man who really baptised Christ, and is, i.e. is represented as being, the same man as the man who baptised Christ in the first picture.[12]

I have now tried to say how we talk and think about things in pictures. The account given so far is incomplete: we have still to see what the truth conditions are for statements about things in pictures, what entitles us to say that a thing in a picture is indeed a horse and grazing or the like. But at least the general character of such statements should be clear. The account of what happens, of what is represented, in a picture, is a description of that picture, and is to be contrasted with the account of the pattern on the canvas, which is a description of the canvas, but rather a prescription for than a description of the picture. I said earlier that the account of the pattern is a description of what constitutes a picture, while the account of the things in the picture is an account of what is constituted by this. We may complete the analogy between representation and reality by substituting 'represent' for 'constitute'. The account of the pattern is a description of what represents a horse in a field; the canvas represents a horse in a field because it is coloured thus; and the account of the things in the picture is a description of what is represented by this.

2. *How a representation can be successful*

An artist who paints a picture of a horse normally wishes to represent it as having certain characteristics, if only those typical of horses. If, in the resultant picture, it has, or is indeed represented as having, these characteristics, the artist has scored a success. Whether such a success has by itself high aesthetic value, we shall consider later; but certainly it seems a prerequisite of success by any more sophisticated mimetic criteria. We must see, then, how it can be secured. In doing so we shall be answering the question left open in the last section: what are the truth conditions of statements describing pictures?

We may begin by distinguishing the remarks 'He has painted a picture of Helen, fairest of women' from 'He has painted a picture of Helen in which he represents her as the fairest of women'. The first remark is true if Helen, the fairest of women, is the person he intended to paint.

A simple way of finding out whom the artist intended to paint, is to ask him, but he cannot give just any answer, or claim that any picture he has painted, no matter what it looks like, is a picture of Helen. On an old-fashioned view of intention, indeed, he could. Philosophers of the past conceived intentions in much the way in which, we saw above,[13] they conceived pleasures and emotions. An intention or volition was a simple act, indescribable but known by introspection: 'He who desires to understand what it is', says Locke, 'will better find it by reflecting on his own mind and observing what it does when it wills, than by any variety of articulate sounds whatever.'[14] Volitions were allowed to cause physical actions or movements of the body, but the connection between cause and effect was contingent, not logical. Hence there would be no logical impossibility in my intending to paint Helen, and there growing under my hands what looks more and more like a picture of a bicycle.

More recent philosophers[15] have rejected this view of intention, and there does seem, in fact, to be a logical connection between what a person intends, or his intention in doing something, and what he does. Helen is a human being, and though for symbolic purposes she could be invested with some non-human attributes, anyone who intends something in his picture to be Helen must intend it to be the same woman as Helen, and hence must try to give it at least some human attributes. And not anything will do as trying to give human attributes. A person cannot try to achieve something unless he has some idea what would help towards or impede the achievement, and he is not trying unless he recognises impediments, and tries to overcome them. A man who is manifestly cutting the lawn cannot claim to be trying to build a boat. And a man who is drawing something that looks like a bicycle, and does not recognise that it looks like a bicycle and not a human being, or recognising this does not do anything about it, cannot claim to be drawing a human being.

To say, then, that a picture is of the individual the artist intends is not to say that the artist can claim that any picture is of anything. On the other hand a picture can be of a certain individual without its subject having, in it, all the attributes the individual really has. Suppose I commission you to paint a picture of my beautiful, chaste young wife, and you paint a picture the woman in which is represented as a repulsive harlot, and hang this in the Academy. I might try to have the law on you, and you will not escape by saying: 'The woman in my picture is a repulsive harlot; the wife of the plaintiff is not a repulsive harlot; so my picture cannot be a picture of the plaintiff's wife': if you could, no libel action would ever succeed.

This may seem obvious, but the point was missed by Descartes in his principal proof of the existence of God.[16] Descartes conceived ideas as mental pictures. He held that an idea must have a cause, and the cause of an idea must be of a power or intelligence proportionate to its object, to what we might call the thing in it. Thus a man with an idea of a nuclear reactor must be a considerable scientist. Now Descartes had an idea of a perfect being, God. The cause of this idea must itself be a perfect being, i.e. not just Descartes but God himself. Descartes clearly failed to distinguish between having an idea of a perfect being, and having an idea of something which in that idea appears as perfect. If God had been represented in Descartes' idea as omnipotent, omniscient and the rest, Descartes' idea would indeed have been the product of a powerful intelligence, just as if Helen is represented in a picture as the fairest of women, the picture must be the product of no mean artist. But any dunce can form an idea of a perfect being, in which the perfection of that being does not appear at all clearly, just as any dauber can paint a picture of Helen in which her beauty does not appear at all clearly.

This brings us to the question: when is it true to say that the artist has represented Helen as the fairest of women? When is it true to say that something in a picture has a specified attribute? The simplest answer here seems to be correct. A thing in a picture has an attribute, or is represented as having an attribute, when it appears to have that attribute to a beholder.

It follows from this that a thing's having an attribute in a picture is something relative, not something absolute. An object is represented as a man, or as brown-haired, or as angry, only relative to a beholder or set of beholders. I do not think this consequence will be found embarrassing in practice. It may turn out that a picture is a mimetic success in one age or society but not in another, but it will not turn out that whether a picture is a mimetic success is a hopelessly subjective question.

A thing in a picture has, in that picture, the attributes which it appears to have. What is meant by appearing here, and how can a thing in a picture (not a piece of canvas or patch of paint but a thing represented by a painted canvas) appear to have attributes? It will help us to understand this if we consider a couple of analogous cases, seeing things in mirrors, and seeing things in real life.

We see things in mirrors, and may attribute properties to those things. The properties a thing has in a mirror are, like the properties of a thing in a picture, properties it appears to have; but they are not properties it is represented as having. The object does not exist in the mirror, but neither is it represented in the mirror: it is reflected in the mirror, and the properties it appears to have are the properties it is reflected as having. And there are other differences.

Things in pictures are represented in one way by the canvas, in another by the artist who colours the canvas. Things in mirrors are reflected in one way by the mirror; but what reflects them as the artist represents his subjects? The objects themselves. They do not, of course, reflect themselves deliberately, any more than rivers wash away villages deliberately; they do, however, play the role in reflection which the artist plays in representation. They send off light rays which strike the surface of the mirror and are reflected from it. In doing this they make themselves apparent to beholders at various points. The artist makes the things in his picture apparent by colouring the canvas. An object does not make itself apparent in a mirror by colouring the mirror. The rays of light do not build up an image on the surface of the mirror, and there is no image apart from perceivers. Mirrors are, in a slightly eerie way, blank until perceivers or cameras with lenses come into the room. But the object does give the mirror a sort of ability to make it, the object, apparent to observers at various angles.

We see things not only in mirrors and pictures, but in real life. Real life is not, of course, something analogous to a picture or mirror, though there is perhaps something analogous to these in real life, namely the retinal image; but that for the moment we may leave aside. Clearly in ordinary seeing, as in seeing in mirrors, the object itself plays the part which the artist plays in the case of pictures. As the object itself sends its rays to the mirror, so the object itself sends its rays to the perceiver. In so doing it is not, as Locke may have thought, representing itself, but rather presenting itself, or directly appearing. The word 'representation' suits what the artist does, because the artist presents the things he paints in accordance with a prescription or formula made up by himself. He himself works out a pattern which he imparts to the canvas, and how the things in the picture appear depends on this. But in the way in which the appearance of things in pictures depends on a pattern worked out by the artist, the appearance of things in reality depends on the pattern they actually exemplify. Hence they should be said rather to be presented than represented. Things in mirrors also appear in accordance with their actual properties but inasmuch as they appear in mirrors we may say that they appear indirectly. A thing which is seen in a mirror is seen indirectly. But by contrast with that, a thing seen in the ordinary way is seen directly or appears directly. Hence although we may, if we like, say that the properties we attribute to things seen in real life are properties they appear to have, the properties which such a thing appears to have are the properties which it is directly perceived to have, which it is directly apparent as having,[17] which, we might say, it manifests itself as having or manifestly has.

I set aside retinal images a moment ago because philosophers since the time of Berkeley have held that they are irrelevant to the philosophical discussion of vision. The reasons they give, however, are not always convincing. Berkeley himself held, paradoxically enough, that they are tangible objects.[18] It is more usual to say simply that we do not see them.[19] But that is inadequate, for it might still be that whatever we do see, we see in a retinal image. If you have a good mirror, you do not see it, but only things in it. Indeed, when we see things represented in a picture, we do not see the canvas. It is not possible at the same time to see the size, shape and colour of a patch of paint, and the size, shape and colour of the thing in the picture which that patch represents. But in the sense in which we see a picture when we see things in it, it could be held without logical absurdity that we see, and always see, retinal images.

A better argument for leaving retinal images out of account is that when we see anything our eye is constantly moving and scanning, and the retinal image is constantly changing.[20] This argument suggests that there is not a correlation between the state of our retina and what we can see, closely similar to the correlation between the pattern on a canvas and the represented scene; it does not of course show, nor is it easy to believe, that there is not an exact correlation of some sort between the features a thing can be seen to have and the effect it has on the eye.

The comparison with seeing things in mirrors and in real life shows, I hope, that it is natural to talk of things in pictures appearing, and appearing to have definite features, but more remains to be said. When a thing sends its rays to a mirror, that it appears in a certain way to the beholder is something which can be explained by an expert on catoptrics, the study of mirrors. When a thing sends its rays to the eye, that it appears in a certain way to the perceiver is something which can be explained by an expert on optics. Who is to explain how it is that when an artist colours canvas a certain way, what he paints appears to have certain qualities? The drawing-master? Yes, but the philosopher may contribute something too.

Philosophers have sometimes toyed with the idea that there are some characteristics the presence of which can actually be seen, discerned by sight alone, and others whose presence we have in some way to infer from the former. Thus Berkeley says: 'The passions which are in the mind of another are of themselves to me invisible. I may nevertheless perceive them by sight, though not immediately, yet by means of the colours they produce in the countenance. We often see shame or fear in the looks of a man, by perceiving the changes of his countenance to red or pale'.[21]

Berkeley I think runs together two distinctions which it is in fact important to keep separate: the distinction between what can and what cannot be ascertained simply by the sense of sight, and the distinction between what we can tell straight off by sight and what we infer. Much of what we knew about the moon until recently we knew just by the sense of sight. By sight we ascertained its hue and brightness, its two-dimensional outline shape, and its angular size. That it has the characteristics thus ascertained, that it is white, circular and thirty minutes of arc across, comes into the description of it under which it affects our eyes, and it is reasonable to say that a characteristic is strictly visible only if it does come into this description of whatever object has it, only if it makes a difference to the effect of that object on the eye. We cannot tell just by sight that a man is an old friend, because it is not as an old friend but as a coloured expanse that he affects our eye. Nor that he is smiling. Perhaps the curve of his lips comes into that description of his face under which we are affected by it; but to smile is not just to curve your lips thus but to do so in a certain frame of mind and on account of certain things, and why a man is curving his lips is irrelevant to how they affect our eyes. But although colour, outline shape and angular size are thus strictly visible characteristics, it does not follow that they are the only characteristics a thing can strictly be seen to have, or that other characteristics are inferred from them.

To tell that a thing has a characteristic, even to tell that it is vermilion or indigo, is not just to expose your retina to it. You must also apply a concept. Whether some concepts are satisfied can be ascertained by sight alone in the way just indicated, and whether other concepts are satisfied cannot. Among the latter we should probably include concepts of three dimensional shapes. People with two eyes have indeed depth vision up to a point—about five feet away; but that a tin of soup thirty feet away is a cylinder, or that an object a hundred feet away has the three-dimensional shape of a man, cannot be ascertained just by sight. Still less is it ascertainable that the stuff in this glass is water or gin. Gin differs from water in that it can be made to boil by less heat, and in that it can make us drunk, and such aptitudes to affect and be affected by other things do not enter into the description of the contents of the glass as an influence on the retina. Similarly, if I was right in suggesting that we conceive a dog as a thing which behaves in a certain way, constituted by a certain formation of flesh and bone, we cannot ascertain just by sight that a thing satisfies the concept of a dog.

Nevertheless we often apply to things we see, straight off and without any inference or deliberation, concepts the satisfaction of which cannot be ascertained just by sight, and conversely we often do not and cannot apply concepts the satisfaction of which is so ascertainable. We can usually tell straight off that an object is a man, that the stuff on his hand is blood, that he is in pain. We are not usually aware of the outline shape, or even, in a sense, of the colour, of familiar objects seen under good conditions of observation. And that, although it is fairly obvious that we tell that the thing before us is a man and in pain by his strictly visible characteristics, by colours and outline shapes.

As a first step to understanding this, let us consider colour. I said in the last chapter that in general to see a thing is to perceive it by its colour. (By that I did not mean to suggest that we see colours directly and physical objects only indirectly, as if the colours somehow got between us and them. What it is to perceive indirectly has been said above. Perceiving a thing by its colour is like striking a thing by a blow. It is not the case that we directly strike blows and that we strike tables and enemies only indirectly: the blow does not come between us and the table.) Similarly when we tell by sight that a thing is a certain colour we do so by the colour of the thing; and we may distinguish the colour by which we perceive from the colour we perceive the thing to have.

This is a difficult point to make about ordinary vision, but becomes intelligible as soon as we consider pictures. If I look across my lawn on a sunny afternoon, I can tell by sight that it is an even green. That is the colour it really is, and the colour I am assured it is by sight. If I look at a naturalistic picture of a lawn on a sunny afternoon, I can again tell by sight that it is an even green. I am assured of this by the colours the artist has applied to the canvas, and it is extremely unlikely that he has applied to the canvas an even grass green. (If he had, I should probably have been assured of the presence not of a lawn, but of a lake.) Rather he has used grey, brown, yellow, 'the colour of an old violin', almost anything but the colour the beholder is assured the grass in the picture has.

How, then, am I assured of the colour of the real lawn? Aestheticians who talk of the lost innocence of the eye[22] perhaps imagine that an infant is first conscious of patches of grey, yellow, old violin colour etc., then learns to infer from these to grass-green and finally forgets the original colours. This seems not merely implausible but impossible. To put the matter at its easiest, the infant would have to pick out patches as exemplifying colours he knows, i.e. of which he has concepts. If he knows the colour yellow, say, he must have derived the concept from physical objects he has already been able to identify, such as coloured bricks, daffodils. But to have the concept is to be able to tell, in a variety of lights, whether a physical object really is yellow. The most innocent child with the concepts of yellow and green would apply the latter to sunlit grass. And in general, the colour of which we are aware when we look at a thing is the colour we think it is. Our colour concepts (though they are not, perhaps, the most important in this respect) enable us to be aware of things which can affect the eye. If a man who has the concept of green is aware of a patch of sunlit grass, his awareness (if it is not some more sophisticated belief) just is awareness that it is green, and if he has no concept applicable to the patch he cannot be aware of it at all.

The artist, then, cannot read off from the real lawn the colours he must use for his picture. Sometimes he must find them by experiment, mixing paints until he hits on a good match. An experienced artist may be able to look at the lawn and say straight off what are good colours to use, but that may be compared with a doctor's ability to tell at a glance what disease is afflicting you. It is an indication that the artist does not copy the colours by which we see things that what hue he uses matters less than what variations in paleness and darkness. Different parts of the lawn affect our eyes with different force, according as different amounts of light fall on them, and the artist seeks a pattern for his canvas which will affect us similarly. To take up a comparison offered earlier, a thing manifests a single colour, i.e. a single general ability to affect the eye, by affecting the eye in different ways, somewhat as a carpenter aboard a rolling ship exercises a single ability, the ability to knock a nail in straight, by striking different blows. He is not exercising a different skill each time he strikes a different blow, and neither is the grass a different colour, now yellow, now grey etc., each time we tell it is green by a different effect on us.

A similar account may be given of how we tell linear size and three dimensional shape. We tell that a thing is the size and shape of a man by its colour, outline shape and angular size or ratio in size to other things, its 'strictly visible characteristics'. Our concepts of shapes like a cube or the shape of a man, however, are probably more primitive than our colour concepts, and certainly function in the same way. A person with the concept of a cube is typically a person whose awareness of a colour variation extending in a hexagonal outline shape just is the thought that the thing before him is a cube. To acquire such a concept is to acquire the ability to be made conscious of things in this way, by a range of strictly visible characteristics—we tell, for instance, that a table-top is rectangular by a variety of rhomboid outlines. And hence an artist can make it clear that a thing in his picture is the shape of a book by a patch of paint with an outline shape by which we tell in ordinary vision that something is a book; or that two trees in his picture are the same height but one a hundred yards behind the other, by patches which subtend angles at the beholder in the same ratio in which two such real trees would at the point from which the picture is painted.

How does the artist do this? The rules of perspective are precisely rules for helping him. But cannot the artist who is painting, say, a seated woman, just look at the seated woman? The relevant outline shapes are indeed ascertainable by sight, but to ascertain them we must know them. Perhaps few people have the concept of the outline shape of a cylinder like a penny or a cigarette seen sideways. Very few have the concept of the outline shape of a seated woman's knees at a distance of six feet; still fewer of the outline shapes exemplified by those parts of her skin or dress which affect the eye with the same force. So although an artist may come in time to tell by looking what shapes to use, he will probably have to begin by experimenting until he hits on the right shape (or by copying from another picture). In general we either do not have or do not apply concepts of the outline shapes of things we see; though sometimes, for instance when the conditions of observation are bad, we do tell straight off that a thing has a certain outline, and conjecture about its three-dimensional shape.

When we come to concepts like those of flesh, a man, grief, the case is more complex. We would normally say that we tell a thing is made of a certain sort of stuff, or that it is an artefact or living thing of a certain sort, by the colour, three-dimensional shape and linear size it can be seen to have. Similarly we usually tell a person's state of mind by the expression on his face, that is, by the three-dimensional pattern exemplified by his face. (It may be remarked that though expression is now contrasted with representation, the word came into aesthetics in this context, the context of assessment by mimetic, not expressionist, criteria. Winckelmann defines it thus: 'In art, the term *expression* signifies imitation of the active and passive states of the mind and body, and of the passions as well as the actions. In its widest sense it comprehends action; but in its more limited meaning it is restricted to those emotions which are denoted by looks and the features of the face.'[23] The emotions expressed in a picture are thus those made apparent by the physical features of the faces in it, that is, they are those represented.)

But should we say, then, that mental states and the like are normally inferred from the bodily characteristics things are perceived to have? Sometimes we do ponder over a man's expression and try to make inferences from it: is he meditating treachery? or on the edge of a nervous breakdown. But often we tell straight off. As when a person knows the shape of a fan, awareness of an object may simply be the thought that it is fan-shaped, so, for a man with such a concept of a dog as most of us have, awareness of a certain formation of flesh and bone under good conditions of observation just is the thought that it is a dog. Similarly awareness of a face with what we call an agonised expression may itself be the opinion that the man is in pain. And when this is so, when our awareness of the shape of the dog or face is awareness or belief that the thing is a dog or the man in pain, we are not aware what the shape is by which we tell this. That is why we sometimes remember that there was a dog in the yard but not what sort of dog, or that a person was in pain but not how he screwed up his face; and why a painter whose aim is to make clear the mental characteristics of the people in his picture has a wide choice of means, and need not be highly naturalistic or detailed in his treatment of their physical features.

It is indeed here, we may think, that the mimetic painter chiefly shows his skill. We tell that a man in a picture is a man and happy or meditating treachery by the overt physical characteristics he has in the picture, the shape of his mouth and so on; and a painter by emphasising or giving prominence to some such characteristics, and playing down others which point in wrong directions, can enable a beholder to tell straight off that a person in the picture is in a state of mind, to which in ordinary experience we usually have to infer. Though it may also be an achievement to leave us guessing, if it is then clear to us that an expression or movement is indeed enigmatic. We might praise Giotto's picture of the betrayal of Christ[24] because it is immediately plain that Judas is in a very fell state of mind; and the *Mona Lisa* because the expression of the face is puzzling, and invites us to try to draw deductions.

It is sometimes wondered how far it is a matter of convention what represents what, or what attributes a thing in a picture has for a given public. There certainly can be convention in painting: it is conventional, perhaps, to represent St Peter with keys; but it is, I think, on the whole misleading to say that representation depends heavily on convention.

It is hardly a matter of convention what size, shape or colour a thing in a picture appears to be. It appears to be a definite size, shape and colour in accordance with laws of perspective which have a demonstrable basis in nature. It can be shown, for instance, what angle an object will subtend to any observer at a given point, and with what force light from it will arrive there. At the same time it may be a matter of convention whether we use ordinary perspective, or inverted perspective as Byzantine artists sometimes did,[25] and different societies may favour more or less extensive use of techniques like perspective; for too much naturalism may confuse the beholder or prevent him from discerning specially interesting characteristics like dispositions to behave and states of mind.

A beholder discerns these in a picture by just the same more overt characteristics of shape, size etc., by which he would discern them in real life. In different societies the same things have been somewhat differently conceived, and the satisfaction of the same concept has been differently manifested. I give a couple of crude examples. In one society horses are chiefly used in battle, and the things recognised as horses are usually seen in a military context, so an artist who wishes to make clear that the animal in his picture is a horse gives it the shape of a small, fierce, rearing horse with bared teeth. In another society horses are widely used in agriculture, and the outline shapes by which beholders have learned to tell that a thing is a horse, are those exhibited by large, slow, patient horses at the plough. A beholder in this second society will find equestrian pictures in the first unclear or unsatisfactory. Again, in one society a suppliant seizes the great man's beard to prevent him giving the jerk of refusal: in another such a movement would be an unheard of impertinence, and suppliants stand with a humble stoop. Obviously artists in the two societies must give their figures different shapes or attitudes to make it clear that the same concept is being satisfied, that of supplication. I do not think, however, that we should conclude that the representation of horses or suppliants is conventional. A convention suggests something arbitrary, which you can change if you wish. A society cannot change its concepts of things like horses, its procedures of supplication and the like, without changing its whole way of life. Similarly the facial expressions by which people are discerned to be pleased, offended, members of a social class etc., may vary from society to society, but are not arbitrarily selected and cannot be changed at will.

Again, in some societies concepts are important which are completely lacking in others. One society may attach value to martial

ferocity, another to royal dignity, another to mystical contemplation. The ambitious artist will try to give figures in his pictures
qualities of this sort; and his pictures may be quite unintelligible to
beholders from another society. A modern Englishman may find it
difficult to see what quality the Pantocrator at Daphni is represented
as having; impossible to say what quality some Buddhas are represented as having. It would be extremely superficial to explain such
differences in style by saying that Byzantine art and Oriental art
are very conventional.

But although what appears in a picture thus depends in a way,
if not on convention, at least on the beholder's habits of thought,
in another way, of course, it depends wholly on the pattern applied
to the canvas. This pattern is worked out by the artist, and his
mimetic art is primarily his capacity to work out such patterns, to
work out prescriptions or formulae for pictures. The art of the landscape painter is the ability to work out prescriptions for representing
landscapes; the art of the portrait painter is the ability to work out
prescriptions for representing sitters; and so on. This is the meaning
of the scholastic definition of art, *recta ratio factibilium*,[26] a correct
account of things which are made—a definition which looks back
to the Aristotelian idea that the various arts, medicine, architecture
etc., are *logoi*, accounts of, or formulae for, the things to which they
give rise, health, a house etc.[27]

It should be observed that in building up a prescription for a
picture, an artist is not working from a mental image he already has
of the represented scene. He may, of course, have before his eyes in
reality the scene he wishes to represent; but until he has started to
think how he is going to colour the canvas, he has no image in his
mind of the represented scene, and his working out of the prescription
is itself the building up of a mental image.

This is a point eloquently developed by Croce[28] and Collingwood,[29]
who indeed went on to identify the image built up in the artist's
mind with the work of art itself;[30] but since mental images are a
notorious centre of philosophical controversy, we ought to see that
there are in fact grounds for calling the artist's prescription a mental
image.

The old idea was that a mental image is something like an ordinary
physical image in that it is a variously coloured expanse, but unlike
it in that it is in the mind, not in physical space, and seen by the
soul directly, without the use of sense-organs. This idea seems in-
coherent. How can a coloured expanse be seen without eyes? And
how can there be a coloured expanse except in physical space? Ryle

suggested that having a mental image of a visible object is thinking what it would be like to see that object in reality.[31] In this way he got rid of non-spatial coloured expanses; but his account, when examined closely, looks like a description of a man, not so much imagining or visualising a visible object, as thinking how he would enact the part (as it might be at a party) of a person seeing that object. Ryle's suggestion, in effect, is that to imagine a scene is to think how you would represent a person seeing it. An obvious simplification is the one suggested here:[32] that to imagine a scene is to think how you would represent the scene itself, and that an artist's way of imagining a scene is thinking how he would represent it on canvas. (Another person might be thinking how he would describe it in speech.)

It is appropriate to call the pattern the artist works out a mental image, or an image in his mind, because we often say that something is in a man's mind if he intends it, or considers bringing it about in reality. When an artist works out his prescription, the picture is in his mind in this sense, and the pattern, the variation in colour, insofar as it does not yet extend over the canvas but is still being contemplated—contemplated in the sense in which a journey you are thinking of making is being contemplated by you—may be called a mental picture or mental image.

But although there is thus such a thing as the artist's mental representation, the work of art as it is in his mind, it seems wrong to call this the real work of art or 'work of art proper'.[33] A picture in an artist's mind stands to a picture in a gallery as a murder in a malicious person's mind stands to a murder in a dark alley: in both cases it is the latter which is the real thing, and the former, as I suggested above, should be called rather a possibility than an actuality.

I have now tried to explain how an artist can bring it about that a thing in a picture appears to have various characteristics. This is obviously something artists wish to do; but why is it worth doing? What is the aesthetic value in the achievement, or, to put it differently, why do we like pictures which are successful as representations? Many answers are possible, of which we may look at two.

First, looking at a picture and discerning what is the case in it is an intellectual activity comparable to interpreting a difficult speech or mastering a problem, and as such may be a pleasure. What we think is going on in a picture is or should be determined by factors internal to it, the visible characteristics of the things in it. I say should be, for we can sometimes tell at a glance that a picture represents a well-known scene, e.g. Christ crucified, without it being at all clear from the attitude and expression of the person in the picture that he is being crucified, or offering himself as a sacrifice to God for mankind, or anything else it would be interesting to have made clear. And there may sometimes be a doubt, comparable with though less disturbing than one which, we shall see, arises over the interpretation of a poem, about how far we are going by internal factors, and how far by what we know about the picture or artist, by the setting, and so forth. Still, it is often natural to say that it is clear from the picture what is happening in it; and when that is so and we look attentively and need no ulterior motive for looking, the contemplation is likely to be a pleasure. Aristotle seems to have had this in mind when he said: 'All men delight in representations. An indication of this is what happens in practice. We delight in seeing very detailed images of things which themselves are distressing to see, like the forms of disgusting animals and corpses. The reason is that understanding is very pleasant, not only to academics, but also to ordinary men, though they do less of it. That is why they delight in seeing images: as they contemplate they come to understand, and reason each thing out, e.g. that this is so-and-so. For it it happens that the subject has never been seen before, it is not as a representation that the picture pleases, but by the workmanship or the colour or the like.'[34]

Although a picture which holds the attention of a sophisticated beholder in this way and is a pleasure to understand, has, I think, for that reason alone aesthetic merit, successful representation may be valued also on slightly different grounds. We conceive ordinary things in a variety of ways, are aware of them under a variety of descriptions. A hand, for instance, is what an arm ends in, or a round expanse with five spikes coming out of it; it is also a thing with which we hold other things, or, more precisely, a thing with which we wield weapons such as enable us to defend ourselves against, and secure dominion over, things which are physically stronger than we; it is also a part of the body through which we can convey, in touching another person's hand, affection or reassurance; it is also what we pray or bless with; or what we guide or create with. Some of these descriptions may fairly be called richer, charged with more intellectual content, than others. In real life, though we are often aware of things like hands, it is seldom, perhaps only in unusual or dramatic situations, that we are conscious of them under complex or suggestive descriptions. In a poor picture, such as a child's crude drawing, we recognise something as a hand, but perhaps only as a hand in the sense of a spiky end to an arm; that the figure in the picture has something with which it could weave baskets or play the violin, is not clear from the picture. But anyone interested in the visual arts will be able to recall pictures in which the artist has made him aware of hands under much richer descriptions, enabled him to apply concepts which in ordinary life remain idle.

It is clear that we in practice value pictures which invite us to apply concepts which are subtle or profound. Why we do so will I hope appear in the next chapter, where I discuss feeling and expression: they move us, I shall suggest, in a welcome manner. But although at this point success by mimetic criteria merges with success by criteria which may be called expressionist, we may still say that insofar as an artist contrives to make clear in a picture something which might not be clear in ordinary life, he scores a mimetic success, and his work cannot be void of merit. I mean that if we give certain descriptions of a picture, we are already passing a favourable or unfavourable aesthetic judgement. If I say 'The Madonna in that picture is watchful and tender' I cannot also say that the picture has no good points.

3. *Mimetic criteria and things which are not representations*

A picture, it has been suggested, has aesthetic merit when the beholder can see what is the case in it, especially when seeing this is an exercise of fairly acute understanding. Can similar criteria be applied to things which are not representations, such as men, horses, landscapes in real life, and buildings and works of craftsmanship like Chippendale chairs and Korean vases?[35] The most natural way would be to say that these things also have aesthetic merit if it is clear to the beholder, from their shape, size, colour, movements etc., that they have other less readily visible characteristics, or if the beholder is led, by looking at them, to think of them under unusually rich descriptions.

Medieval aestheticians took this line, and even defined beauty accordingly. Typical scholastic definitions of beauty are *splendor* or *resplendentia formae*. By *splendor* was meant not splendour in the modern sense but something like shining-outness; and a *forma* was not a thing's shape but its nature. Thus a man would have *splendor formae* if his nature as a being with intelligence and feelings was manifest in his visible appearance[7]. Medieval aestheticians, though they recognised the importance of catching the beholder's attention with pleasant visual sensations,[36] thought that our delight in beauty is primarily intellectual. 'The same things', says Aquinas, 'are called beautiful as are called good, but for different reasons. The good is what is aimed at; and hence it is part of what we mean by good, that desire is satisfied by it; but it is part of what we mean by beautiful that desire is satisfied by perception or knowledge of it. Hence those senses have most to do with beauty which have most to do with knowledge, i.e. sight and hearing in the service of reason [that is, when the exercise of them is also the application of a concept]: we talk of beautiful sights and sounds. We do not use the word "beauty" in connection with objects of other senses, or talk of beautiful tastes or smells. It thus appears that the word "beautiful" indicates, as the word "good" does not, a certain ordinance towards our powers of cognition: a thing is called good if it itself pleases, but beautiful if the bare apprehension of it pleases'.[37]

The scholastic theory has been restated in modern times by a number of writers, in English, perhaps most notably by Eric Gill, though his version incorporates ideas which derive not from Aquinas, but, via A. K. Coomaraswamy, from what I call theological aesthetics. Quite independently, however, Kant worked out an aesthetic theory which has affinities with that of Aquinas.[38] Kant too holds that beauty pleases primarily because it satisfies our cognitive faculties. His account may be summarised as follows. In general, when we find we can do something we want to do, we are pleased. Now we all want to have systematic knowledge of the natural world. Systematic knowledge is the sort of knowledge which fills ordinary scientific books, works on botany, zoology, chemistry and so on: it is possible only in a universe of a certain type, one where there are many species and few genera, and where there is a diversity of particular natural laws which can be brought under a few general laws. A beautiful object, according to Kant, is one which pleases because it plainly belongs to such a universe. Typical beautiful objects, he seems to have thought, are flowers. We cannot tell directly that a flower is part of a universe which will satisfy our desire for systematic knowledge, in the way we can tell directly that a hand is part of a man, because we have no concept of such a universe such as we have of a man. But we can tell indirectly, from the quickening effect the flower has on our understanding and imagination. It is a difficult point of exegesis just what Kant supposed this effect to be. As I said earlier,[39] he held that we cannot be conscious of a sensory intake as an object, until we have given it some kind of form. The sensory intake corresponding to a beautiful object is certainly one which it is particularly easy to form, and my own view is that Kant thought its adaptability lay in this, that it will readily provide the content for judgements of many different logical forms—universal, particular, affirmative, negative, hypothetical, disjunctive and so on. Certainly if we are to make judgements of many different logical forms—to judge, for instance, 'All plants contain chlorophyll; some plants cannot stand an English winter; if it does not rain, nothing will grow: anything which is alive is either a plant or an animal or a man' etc., we live in a universe in which systematic knowledge is possible; so if this tulip is such as to give rise, as we might put it, to judgements of many different forms, it will reassure us of this possibility, and thus be an object of what Kant reckons pure aesthetic pleasure.[40]

As Kant himself presents this theory, it differs from the scholastic theory in an important respect. According to Kant, we tell that an object is beautiful by recognising through introspection the effect it has on our cognitive faculties; we do not need any empirical concepts. The scholastics, on the other hand, would probably say that we have to know a form already before we can recognise that it shines out from a particular individual. But this part of Kant's theory (which makes it appear rather formalist than mimetic)[41] is implausible and dispensable. In point of fact, if there is anything peculiarly apt to give rise to judgements of many different types, and reassure us that systematic natural science can make headway, it will be precisely a thing with *splendor formae*, a horse, say, of which the generic animality and specific horsiness are patent.

Here, then, is a way in which mimetic criteria can be applied to things which are not representations. But is such an application profitable? It is easy to provide safeguards against some of the more obvious objections. A thing will not be an aesthetic success because it is plainly black or round, since these are characteristics of the sort by which others should be made plain. Still less will it be beautiful if it is plainly shapeless or deformed. 'Shapeless' is not, like 'oviform', an expression for a shape, but an expression we apply to things when their shape is not at all clear. And according to the criterion we are considering, it must be clear that a thing has characteristics, not that it lacks them. A girl would not be beautiful because you can tell at a glance that she is stupid, since people are called stupid because they lack qualities, not because they have a special quality called stupidity.

This having been said, however, it seems that our criteria are more appropriate in some cases than in others. That an artefact or a man's physical movement is well adapted for the achievement of the end for which it is made, is a characteristic which is not strictly visible, but which may be seen from what is visible, and if it is, the artefact or movement may be aesthetically good. Gill said that the 'only claim' of aeroplanes and spider-webs 'to be called beautiful is on account of the fine and impressive and immediately obvious per-

fection of their functional adaptation';[42] and there is doubtless something in this, though aeroplanes and spider-webs were more alike in
Gill's day than now. Similarly if you know a little about cooking or
carpentry, the movements of a good cook or carpenter at work may
be a source of aesthetic satisfaction. Again, it is an aesthetic merit in
a human face to be expressive: we like faces we call animated, faces
which reflect the thoughts, changes of mood etc., of the persons
whose faces they are. And it would not necessarily be absurd to
justify your admiration of a horse or bull by pointing to its manifest
animality.

On the other hand it seems impossible to assess all design and
decoration by these criteria. Gill thought he could, on the ground
that artefacts are made to be used by people who have mental as well
as physical needs, and will distress their users unless they have some
grace in design and are well decorated.[43] That is true enough; but the
artefacts must then satisfy criteria of grace and good decoration
before they can be said to be well adapted to our spiritual needs. It
will not do to say simply that a Persian carpet pleases us because it
is plainly easy to live with, and is easy to live with because it pleases
us. And it is still more difficult to explain the aesthetic value of sunsets
or mountain scenery by appeal to mimetic criteria. The Alps do not
draw visitors because they are plainly mountains, nor do we gaze at
sunsets because it is obvious that they serve their purpose. To
understand our esteem for many natural phenomena and works of
craftsmanship, we must take in other criteria, for instance those
discussed in the last chapter.

We have now seen one way in which mimetic criteria have been
applied to things which are not representations; another is to hold
that all physical objects are representations after all. Plato puts
forward this idea in the *Republic*: we recognise that there can be
many pictures of a single physical bed made by a carpenter; we
ought to recognise that the many physical beds we see about us are
representations of a single ideal bed, made, so to speak, by God.[44]
Similarly in the *Cratylus* he suggests that the craftsman who wants
to make a good shuttle will fix his attention on the ideal shuttle.[45]
Whether or not Plato seriously thought that a craftsman must or
can see by intellectual intuition an ideal artefact, this idea has
certainly been held in some ages and societies. 'When an artist', said
Giordano of Pisa in 1305, 'makes a painting or a casket, he must
needs have within himself a figure or a casket which is nobler than
the outward one and gives him more delight. And when he has made
his painting, he pays heed to it no longer, but delights in that which

he has within by virtue of his primal knowledge.'[46] According to Coomaraswamy, the same point is constantly emphasised in Hindu aesthetics: 'Only by introspection, certainly not by direct observation, can an image be rightly made' is a characteristic dictum; and (at one here with Collingwood and Croce) Hindu aestheticians regarded physical works of art as representations or reminders of what had been seen by the mind.[47]

Not only can it thus be held that all artefacts are representations, but it has also been held that things like dogs and trees are representations. 'When men are weak at contemplating', says Plotinus, 'they perform actions as shadows of contemplation and knowledge. Contemplating inadequately because of the debility of their souls, they cannot grasp the object of contemplation sufficiently, and being unsatisfied, and longing to see it, they turn to action, in order that they may see with the senses what they could not see with the mind. . . . Everywhere we may identify making and doing either with weakness of contemplation or with an accompaniment of it: weakness, when the agent has nothing beyond what he effects, an accompaniment, when he has something prior to and greater than his product to contemplate.'[48] If we apply this account to human activity, Plotinus is perhaps saying that a man who has, for instance, a concept of a clock as an instrument which will measure time, but feels that this concept lacks content, devises a structure of cog-wheels and weights so that he may behold a clock with his eyes. Plotinus, however, does not restrict his account to men, but thinks he has a model on which to understand all processes whatsoever. The operations of plants, insects and the like, things weak at contemplating, are a substitute for contemplation; such things exist in the first place, in consequence of the Universal Soul's contemplation of the Universal mind, which contains Platonic ideas, and the Soul itself is not a substitute for, but an accompaniment or by-product of, the Mind's contemplation of the One.[49]

This, we may feel, is wild stuff, and we ought to object to the original Platonic suggestion, that as there are many pictures which are representations of a single physical bed distinct from them, so the many physical beds we see around us are representations (or, if we prefer, realisations in space and time) of a single ideal bed distinct from them. The analogy here is ill-drawn. To compare pictures of beds and real beds correctly, we must observe that the statement that something is a picture of a bed may be taken in two ways. It may mean that that which is represented in the picture is a bed, that a bed is represented in the picture, and the claim is then that the picture is of an individual bed, an individual collection of pieces of wood and metal. Or it may be that the subject of the picture is represented as a bed, that a collection of pieces of wood is a bed in the picture; and the claim is then not that the picture is a picture of an individual bed, but simply that it is a picture of a bed. The artist's skill is a capacity to paint a picture of a bed in this latter sense, i.e. not to represent individual bits of wood, but to represent individual bits of wood as a bed. Now the analogue for the carpenter of the painter's individual bed is indeed something individual, but not something ideal or removed from the physical world: it is the bits of wood and metal which he puts together as or makes into a bed. In so doing he realises them in a way, in that he utilises or exploits them; but his skill lies, not in putting together individual bits of wood, but in putting them together as a bed, and he puts them together just as a bed, not as any individual bed. Properly worked out, then, the analogy between pictures of beds and physical beds does not justify the introduction of a transcendent, ideal bed.

We may reach the same conclusion by a slightly different route. We saw that the artist, by colouring canvas, makes it represent a bed. Here the canvas is something particular or individual, but when we say that this canvas coloured thus represents a bed, we mean, not that it represents an individual thing, but that it represents a kind of thing.[50] Similarly the carpenter, by shaping and putting together bits of stuff, makes them constitute a bed; and again, a bed in this context is rather a kind of thing than an individual thing. So we may say that there are not, as Plato thought, two beds, one which painters represent, and one which carpenters represent or realise. There is one thing, a bed; this is not so much an actual as a possible thing; it is a thing it is possible to make in reality or to represent; and an artist works out a formula for representing it while a carpenter works out a formula whereby it can be realised or really constituted.

With the Plotinian doctrines just reviewed, we are in the realm of theological aesthetics. The theological aesthetician regards everything there is as a manifestation, immediate or at one or more removes, of a single ultimate reality, and the systematic can try to deduce the various contents of the universe, the graduated forms of life, art, and matter, as inevitable moments in the progressive articulation and diversification of this one reality. Hegel, if not Plotinus himself, is such a systematiser. Starting from the position that the whole business of art is 'the sensuous representation of the absolute itself', i.e. of the one reality, he proceeds to make the various forms of art, symbolical, classical and romantic, and the various arts, architecture, sculpture, painting, music and poetry, exactly reflect the various stages in that progressive intellectual understanding of the absolute, which he traces in his *Logic*.[51]

This approach to theoretical aesthetics, which is known as essentialism, is clearly disastrous;[52] but it is perhaps worth noticing that Coomaraswamy's Hindu aesthetics, and Gill's theory which is influenced by it, though not systematic, are also theological. Speaking of the kind of non-sensuous intuition which the artist needs, Coomaraswamy says: 'The theory of *rasa* set forth according to Visvanatha and other aestheticians, belongs to totalistic monism. . . . The doctrine of the universal presence of reality is that of the immanence of the Absolute. It is inconsistent with a view of the world as absolute *maya*, or utterly unreal, but it implies that through the false world of experience may be seen by those of penetrating vision (artists, lovers and philosophers) glimpses of the real substrate.'[53] Similarly, though in a less technical idiom, Gill: 'Unless he [the workman] knows what he is making, he cannot make anything. Whether it is a church or a toothpick, he must know what it *is*. . . . And what a thing *is*, what things *are*, and, inevitably, whether they are good or bad, worth making or not, these questions bring him without fail to the necessity of making philosophical and religious decisions'.[54] 'Every person and every people is concerned to lay hold of reality, and . . . all the works of men display this concern. . . . Different peoples and different times display different works because among such peoples and in such times different notions of reality have been accepted.'[55] As a working artist, Gill has a right to our attention, but what he says is open to the philosophical objection that there is no such thing as reality over and above particular things, and no question what things generally are, over and above the questions what a toothpick is, what gamboge is, what meningitis is, what luffing is, and so on.

4

EXPRESSION

1. *Feelings*

Especially since the beginning of the last century, many people have held that what constitutes merit in a work of art is expression of feeling or emotion. The appeal of this view is easy to see. A work of art, we are inclined to say, speaks to the heart, not just to the intellect; to appreciate it, we must feel it; a person who lacks feeling, though he may have as much knowledge of art history as you please, and succeed as a dealer, expert or don, will be aesthetically dead. And our instinct here is confirmed by many poets, painters and composers who have declared that emotion was the starting point of their work: 'All good poetry', says Wordsworth, 'is the spontaneous overflow of powerful feelings.'[1] As for expression, that seems the most appropriate word for the controlled and yet free and creative activity of the artist: he does not describe or report his emotions, like a patient at the psycho-analyst, nor does he simply show them or let them be seen, like an ill-mannered person in company: he expresses them.

For a development of these insights it is natural to look first to those philosophers who have made it their central aesthetic thesis that art or beauty is expression of feeling or emotion. The accounts they offer, however, are disappointing. Collingwood's is perhaps the best and goes something like this.[2] We receive what he calls bare sensa, raw sensations of colour, sound, smell and the like. These sensa are objects of some sort of awareness or feeling, but not, in their raw state, of consciousness. They carry on them an 'emotional charge', a feeling such as pleasure, pain, anger or fear; and the emotional charge is expressed in an involuntary and sometimes even unconscious bodily movement or change, like a grimace, cry or blush. The relation between sensum, emotional charge and expression

is not contingent or causal in the eighteenth-century sense: Collingwood says that a sensum stands to a feeling of pain or the like as
contracting the biceps stands to raising an arm—that is, I suppose,
it is the same thing under a different description, related, perhaps,
as constituent to thing constituted—and the emotional charge stands
similarly to the expression. A sensum comes to be 'dominated by
consciousness'; that is, we become aware of it as an object which we
can then interpret and set in relation to other objects of consciousness; and at the same time we become aware of its emotional charge
as *our* feeling. The sensum and the charge along with it are trans-
formed, or rather formed, by this domination by consciousness, into
an imaginative experience or idea. To that imaginative idea there is
always, and inevitably, a corresponding expression, and such expressions are, in the broadest sense, language or art. According to
Collingwood, the various kinds of language, from infant gestures up
to the language of formal logicians, and the various kinds of art,
are just so many kinds of expression of sensation and emotion thus
dominated by consciousness, and good artists differ from bad in that
they can make themselves more deeply and fully conscious of their
experience.

Now what has become of feelings and expression in this account?
Instead of being distinguished from what we might crudely call
cognitive thoughts, and thus used to bring out the special character of
art, emotions are partly merged with sensa below the level of consciousness and pretty well completely merged with them above it.
Similarly instead of distinguishing expression from the kind of activity
in which some cold fish like a philosopher would engage, Collingwood makes science and philsophy simply levels of expression. For
the rest, that aspect of art in which we are interested is lost to sight
behind cumbersome epistemological machinery made in Königsberg.
If we suppose that objects of which we are conscious are constructed
or formed by us out of raw sensa, then any object of conscious
intuition is a kind of work of art, even a representation or *Vorstellung*
in Kant's terminology, and an account of consciousness generally
will do as an account of art; but if we reject the original supposition,
and believe that many things of which we are conscious, like the
Parthenon and the Matterhorn, came to be and to have the structure
they have independently of us, then some special account of art
will be necessary.

Official expressionist theories being thus unhelpful, we would
do well to consider feelings and emotions directly. What is an
emotional feeling? What is it to be moved emotionally? Until we

have answered these questions, we shall be ill-placed to see what feelings have to do with aesthetic merit.

We may begin by distinguishing feelings from dispositions.[3] Love, hatred, gratitude, pride, are dispositions which may characterise a person over a long stretch of time. It is true to say of a man that he is proud, or that he loves his wife, even when he is asleep, or reading a book, or performing an action the reverse of proud or loving. Anger, fear, depression, gaiety, on the other hand, are not settled characteristics, but rather things felt or experienced on particular occasions. You may go to bed in anger or fear, but can hardly be called angry or afraid when asleep—I leave aside problems about dreams. It might be said of anger, as it is sometimes said of pain, that it does not exist unfelt; whereas pride may exist, i.e. be correctly attributable to a person, unfelt. Feelings, the things of importance to us here, are states like anger and depression, not states like pride and love. It should be recognised, of course, that emotion expressions may be used to attribute dispositions: I may say of a man who is not feeling fear at the moment: 'He goes in perpetual fear of losing all his money.' And conversely a person with a disposition will in certain circumstances feel emotions which may be called after his disposition. A proud man will have certain feelings, different, but both, we might say, proud, towards desirable and towards undesirable men courting his daughters; a man who loves his wife will at times have loving feelings towards her.[4]

Of feelings some, for which we may reserve the word 'emotion', are always or usually directed at things. Anger and fear are emotions in this sense: we feel anger towards people making thoughtless noises when we are trying to get to sleep, fear at the approach of a homicidal maniac. That to which an emotion is thus directed is called its object. It is common to distinguish the object of an emotion from its cause. By the cause of a person's emotion is usually understood the event which disposed him to feel it in appropriate circumstances. Thus Kenny says: 'When the burnt child dreads the fire, the object of his fear is the fire which he is here and now afraid of; but his present fear is the effect of his past experience.'[5] This use of the word 'cause' is a little unnatural;[6] just as the cause of a stick's lighting is a flame applied to it or the like, not its being moved to a dry place and thus rendered capable of being lit, so it is natural to give as the cause of a person's emotion whatever excites that emotion in him or moves him with it, i.e. what angers or frightens him. Still, so long as we remember how the word 'cause' is being used in this context, no confusion need arise.

If a person's emotion is directed towards an object, he must be

aware of that object, and what we are aware of, we are aware of
under some description. When, therefore, we say that someone feels
anger or fear at something, we may give the object under a description under which the person moved thinks of it, or under some other
description. One way of putting this is to say that our language in
speaking of a man's emotions may be intensional or referentially
opaque.[7] If I say 'He is in fear of the ghost' the reference of 'the
ghost' is opaque; I am not committed to holding that there is a ghost.
This indicates (what is anyhow scarcely doubtful) that emotions are
mental states, since intensionality is considered, at least by many, a
distinguishing mark of reports of mental states. The matter, however,
may also be put like this. A distinction is sometimes drawn between
formal and material objects.[8] The material object of Øing is whatever
is in fact Øed; the formal object is what is Øed precisely under the
description under which it is Øable. Thus a mouse or train may be a
material object of hearing, but the formal object of hearing is a
thing which is making a sound or noise. We may adapt this distinction
to objects of emotion. That which excites a person's emotion, under
whatever description we care to apply, is its material object; it is its
formal object under the description (which may well be false or highly
inappropriate) under which the person moved thinks of it. Thus
consider the three remarks: 'He is angry because he has drunk two
glasses of sherry', 'He is angry because you said that Virgil is an
imitative poet', 'He is angry because you, a person of no account,
contradicted him, an eminent professor'. In the third, the word
'because' introduces the formal object of his anger, in the second the
material, and in the first the cause.[9]

The eighteenth-century view was that anything could be the formal
object, in this sense, of any emotion, and if we accept it, there will
be no point in using the expression 'formal object'. The eighteenth-
century view, however, seems arbitrary and mistaken. Aristotle
defined anger and fear by their objects: anger as 'appetition, with
distress, for vengeance on account of an apparent slight to you or
yours by someone with no business to slight you', and fear as 'distress
or disturbance resulting from an appearance of impending evil which
will be destructive or painful'.[10] That, we may think, is on the right
lines. If we are to feel anger or fear towards a thing, it is necessary,
not indeed that the thing should be in fact, but that it should appear
to us to be, a slight or menace. (A tyrant might be rather frightened
than angered by a courtier's insolence; in that case he would take
the courtier's behaviour not just as a slight but as an indication that
there is a conspiracy afoot.)

Part, then, of feeling anger or fear is thinking of something under a certain description; another part is behaving like a man in fear or anger. Here are two reasons for thinking that a man's emotional state is not logically independent of his behaviour. First, a typical use of our concept of anger is to explain shouting, violence and the like, so that to a person who betrays no inclination even to such behaviour, our concept is hardly applicable. Similarly the object of fear is usually something which threatens us with pain, and it belongs to the concept of pain that we try to avoid it. Second, awareness of anything under any description is, in appropriate circumstances, reflected in action. If you are handed something, and are aware it is fragile, you handle it carefully. All the more, then, when we are aware of something under a description under which it is emotionally moving. Although, however, the idea of any emotion is thus in general bound up with an idea of how it is manifested, we sometimes attribute a feeling to a person who gives no sign of it, if there is an object well calculated to excite it and good reason for not betraying it—thus we attribute anger to the man who looks on stonily while the political police ill-treat his mother—just as persistent timorous behaviour may persuade us that a child is frightened of something, even though no description under which it would be frightening seems to fit it.

Is there anything more to anger or fear than thinking of something in a certain way, and behaving appropriately? Some philosophers feel it perverse to deny that there is also an inner feeling, discernible by introspection, but their case is not, I think, made out. True enough, a man sometimes knows better than anyone else what his emotional state is, but he need not know this by introspection; it may simply be that he knows better than we the descriptions under which things appear to him. It is also true that an emotion may involve bodily sensations, feelings of sickness, cold and the like;[11] but these are not so much objects of introspective awareness as themselves awarenesses or modes of awareness of changes and the like in the body, sometimes even of external things. And there is certainly a difference between simulating anger and being angry, but this may sufficiently be traced to the reasons for simulation, and the way in which the object of genuine anger is thought of.

I have been speaking of anger and fear, but a similar account can be given of other emotions such as pity and feelings of desire. The word 'desire' covers a good deal more than emotions, but we do have feelings of desire directed towards specific objects. When on a hot walk I desire beer, I probably betray an inclination to try to get beer, and my mind also dwells on the stuff: I think of it, perhaps, as cold and wet in just the way the walk is hot and dry. Similarly if you feel sexual desire for Amaryllis, you think of her as pleasant to sport with. Thoughts of the sort involved in feelings of sexual jealousy are vividly described by Spinoza in *Ethics*, III, 35 scholium.[12]

It is clear that there is a wide variety of descriptions under which things may move us in various ways. Is there any way of distinguishing descriptions under which a thing is moving from descriptions under which it is not, or are we under the influence of at least some weak emotion all the time? It depends on what we contrast emotion with. If with impersonal detachment we might say: a thing is an object of emotion insofar as it is thought of under a description under which it is directly or indirectly harmful or beneficial to ourselves.[13] A thing would be indirectly harmful or beneficial, if it was a source of good or evil to some person or thing whose interests we have made our own. Pity can thus be accommodated, for when we pity someone we precisely make our own the interests of a person in a bad situation. Alternatively, since we contrast emotional with rational conduct, we might say (approaching an Aristotelian position[4]) that to feel an emotion is to think of something under a description which diverges in certain ways from that under which a rational or prudent man would think of it. Thus to feel fear is to think of it under a description under which it is more frightening than it appears to a rational person; to be angry is to consider something more of a slight than a rational person would.

So much, for the moment, on feelings directed towards objects. Some feelings, for instance depression[14] (here different from grief), and gaiety, have no single definite object. There seems also to be objectless feelings of anger, fear and the like. Let us call these undirected emotional states moods. A mood is not, any more than a directed emotion, an object of introspection. To be in a mood is not to be conscious of a special feeling in yourself, but to be conscious of other things in a special way. You notice things which you normally overlook, and *vice versa*; you have sensations you would not normally have, and the reverse; and what you would normally think of in one way, you think of in a different. Thus if a man is depressed, his wife, of whom he is fond, appears plain and stupid. A day on which he would normally go out gladly seems too cold or cloudy for a walk. He does not hear the singing of the birds but only the noise made by his, therein defective, refrigerator. While if he is in a gay or cheerful mood, it is just the opposite. If he is in a bad temper, though there is not one single thing at which his anger is directed, many things appear to him under descriptions under which they are irritating; the telephone, for instance, as a source of noise instead of a means of communication. And if he bumps into something, it will probably hurt more than usual. As for the person in a mood of fear, every shadow is a concealment for something unpleasant, every sound an indication of hostile forces abroad. It may be added that we can explain in this sort of way, what might otherwise seem puzzling, directed fear which has apparently no real object, like a man's fear of a ghost which does not in fact exist, but about which he has been told stories: the object of his fear is not so much a non-existent or fictitious ghost as a room or the like under the false description 'haunted'.

Although, then, moods are in a sense objectless, being in a mood is still, just as much as having a feeling directed at an object, a matter of thinking of things under certain descriptions. It follows that feelings generally are themselves accurately describable in words. Words like 'anger' and 'depression' are indeed generic in character: they are not expressions for specific feelings in the way in which 'equilateral triangle', 'regular tetrahedron' are expressions for specific shapes. Rather, each covers a perhaps unlimited number of similar feelings. We need not conclude, however, in Mrs Langer's words, that 'language is a very poor medium for expressing our emotional nature. It merely names certain vaguely and crudely conceived states, but fails miserably in any attempt to convey the ever-moving patterns, the ambivalences and intricacies of inner experience, the interplay of feelings with thoughts and impressions, memories and echoes of memories, transient fantasy, or its mere runic traces, all turned into nameless, emotional stuff'.[15] Why should it fail? Is the inner experience of Pierre Bezukhof after a thousand pages still nameless emotional stuff? Many novels are prized precisely because the author succeeds in giving extremely detailed accounts of his characters' emotional lives, and he succeeds in the way I have tried to indicate, by saying what things they are aware of under what descriptions, and how they react. Proust is outstanding in this field; in *Le temps retrouvé* he says that the secret is to recognise that every word a man speaks or gesture he makes is surrounded and set off by a great number of things which have no logical connection with it, but of which he is aware at the time;[16] by describing these, as they appear, the novelist makes the mental states of his characters more intelligible to us even than our own.[17]

2. *Two aesthetic emotions*

Although all human feelings are grist to the artist, there are two which have a special interest for the aesthetician: the pure aesthetic emotion to which Bell and other formalists appeal, and amusement, or whatever it is which we are made to feel by artists in comedy.

When we find a writer claiming that all aesthetic appreciation is a matter of feeling one single emotion, and then proving quite unable to give any account in words of what this emotion is like, it is tempting to say that there is no specifically aesthetic emotion, that all the emotions we feel in connection with works of art are at most variants of emotions we feel over other things. But room can in fact be found for a special aesthetic emotion. We feel an emotion if we think of something under some special description, typically one under which it is harmful or beneficial to ourselves. The descriptions 'pleasant to look at', 'pleasant to listen to' are descriptions under which a thing is a force for good in our lives. They are not the only descriptions under which we can think of pieces of music or design. We can think of a statue as a landmark, a tapestry as a draught-excluder, music as an innocent occupation for young ladies. So if we do think of a thing as satisfying the criteria discussed in Chapter 2, we may well be moved by it, and moved in a peculiarly aesthetic way. The behaviour which goes with thinking of a thing thus is looking at or listening to it attentively; and such behaviour people exhibit. There are grounds, then, for agreeing that there is a pure aesthetic emotion, and one directed towards the objects towards which people claim it is directed, good patterns and pieces of music.

Do we feel this emotion while enjoying patterns and music? Presumably we can, if, as seems to be the case, a man still feels desire for beer while enjoying a pint, and still feels sexual desire while enjoying an embrace.

A suggestion may be made here about the words 'beauty' and 'beautiful'. The aesthetician may sometimes find it convenient to take 'beauty' as meaning simply whatever constitutes aesthetic merit, and say that beauty stands to aesthetics as goodness stands to ethics; but the English word 'beautiful' (and the same perhaps holds for *pulcher*, if less for καλός, *beau*, *schon*), is not in fact used very freely. We do not call good novels or plays beautiful, hesitate to call beautiful a landscape by Van Gogh or a drawing by Leonardo. We call girls beautiful, and apart from that we apply the word least reluctantly to good pieces of design—well-shaped vases, successful colour combinations and the like—and to pieces of music which are pleasant but not otherwise very moving—to light bits of Mozart more readily than to *Fidelio*. Now in general, to things which are pleasant or distressing we often apply, not just the words 'pleasant', 'distressing', but, depending on the kind of pleasure or distress, more specific words cognate with words for emotions. Something which it is unpleasant to hear, like a pneumatic drill or a strident speaker, we call irritating. A forest fire which it would be extremely unpleasant to feel we call frightening. A girl it would be pleasant to kiss we call desirable. If, then, we use the word 'beautiful' of a pattern or piece of music it would be a pleasure to follow, that suggests that it is, in this restricted use, an emotion-word like 'irritating', 'frightening', and the emotion with which it is connected will be, of course, the pure aesthetic emotion.

Although some modern critics[18] speak as if literature, to have merit, must deal with serious moral questions in a serious manner, in fact a number of literary works, such as the *Thesmophoriazousae*, *Pickwick Papers*, are prized because they liberate us from cares and amuse us. Similarly with some pictures, like Thurber's drawings, and sensitive listeners can extract amusement from pieces of music which contain musical jokes. The judgement that a thing is amusing or, as we call it, funny, simply as it stands seems to be an aesthetic judgement. It is, at least, more akin to the judgement 'That is beautiful' or 'ugly' than to the judgement 'That is annoying' or 'sad'. The aesthetician, then, has particular reason to say something about amusement.

At first sight amusement looks like a directed emotion very similar to anger or fear.[19] It is something we feel on particular occasions towards particular objects (though we may, of course, be in a mood to be amused), and the things which amuse us, or which we deem funny, are not so very different from the things which anger or alarm us. The look on a man's face may be funny, frightening or annoying, and quite similar looks (betraying, perhaps, different sorts of idiocy) can move us in these different ways. And laughter is an expression of amusement as tears are of grief.

There are, however, differences. We saw that a thing tends to be an object of emotion if it appears as a source of good or evil to ourselves or those whose interests we have made our own. Amusement, in contrast, seems to go with an attitude of detachment or disengagement. When we think something funny, we usually do not relate it to ourselves. When we laugh at ourselves it is by, so to speak, stepping aside from ourselves; and when we laugh at someone else, so far from making his interests our own, we are unsympathetic.

Again, amusement seems to be more intellectual than ordinary emotions. We are often inclined to impute anger or fear to an animal, sometimes even feelings of affection, jealousy or pride, but amusement we impute only to human beings. And a sense of humour is thought to be part of intelligence: if a man is completely humourless, can

never see comedy in anything, then however clever, learned or skilled
he may be, we are reluctant to call him intelligent. Kant connected
humour with intelligence, but inadequately. He said that we are
amused when an expectation that we shall have to exert our intellectual powers in no ordinary way, is suddenly brought to nothing; he
does not distinguish cause and object, but his meaning is clearly that
this sort of frustration is the formal object of amusement.[20] His
account holds, perhaps, for shaggy dog stories, with which, indeed,
he illustrates it, but will hardly cover amusement at caricatures, or at
literary characters like Lady Bracknell and the Mrs Bennet of *Pride
and Prejudice*.

A more subtle and penetrating analysis is offered by Plato. He
explains amusement as a sort of pleasure or joy we feel when a person
towards whom we are in general well disposed, holds an opinion
about his own character and intellectual attainments which is false
but has no dire consequences.[21] Plato's account brings out well the
mixture of benevolence and malicious triumph in amusement, and
does some justice to our feelings towards Malvolio and Don Quixote,
but perhaps applies best to humour in the service of satire.

E. F. Carritt argued that humour which has aesthetic merit is the
expression of failure to express emotion.[22] This, as it stands, is
rather too obviously an attempt to stretch the expressionist formula
to cover all forms of art, and it is implausible to say that the novels
of P. G. Wodehouse, for instance, are expressions of failure to express
emotion; but emotion has more to do with humour than appears
from Plato's account. Emotion which is grotesque, which is disproportionate to its object or cause, tends to be funny. If a person feels
anger or fear towards something quite inoffensive, or if he is thrown
into a mood or rage or gloom by some trivial happening, we may be
amused. When we are amused by an animal, real or in a picture, it is
often because we anthropomorphise it, see it as having an emotion
which would be disproportionate in a human being. And if we are
amused by a weird piece of amateur art, or by over-elaborate pre-
cautions against burglars or draughts or the like, the real target of
our amusement may be the feelings of the person responsible.

In handling a topic like humour we should aim less at providing a
single account which will cover everything, than at illuminating a
central or prominent area. Many cases of amusement can, I think, be
explained in the way just indicated: we are thinking of someone as
moved by disproportionate emotion. We need intelligence for this,
since it takes intelligence, what Aristotle called *phronesis*,[4] to tell
what emotion is proportionate in a given situation. And being moved

disproportionately is not wholly separate from holding a false opinion about yourself: Lady Bracknell's unwillingness to let her daughter 'marry into a cloakroom and form an alliance with a parcel' though chiefly funny because she is transferring to the cloakroom and parcel feelings a normal object of which would be human beings, also reflects her idea of her own social importance. We should add the qualification that a good man is unlikely to be amused by someone whose disproportionate emotion brings him considerable good or evil. A man who is made ill by fear of what is not fearful is an object rather of pity than of amusement; and if a man loves a wife we might consider unlovely (perhaps she is without beauty, wit or health), and leads with her a life of unbroken bliss, laughter at his expense may sound a little forced.

3. *Feelings and objects of aesthetic appraisal*

We must now see how feelings can be bound up with things we view and assess aesthetically. It may look at first as if there is a formidable problem here. We call pieces of music, landscapes and the like sad or cheerful. But surely only a person can be sad or cheerful: how then can we apply such emotion-words to works of art and to inanimate nature?[23]

This is a serious problem only if we accept the narrow view mentioned in Chapter 1, that if the same word is to be applied to a number of different things, it must be on the ground that they are similar or have some characteristic in common. We saw then one alternative way of using words, and must now recognise another. A word may be applied to a number of different things which are quite dissimilar, if they are all related, in one way or another, to something to which the word applies in a primary fashion. Thus take the word 'healthy',[24] in its primary use it applies to a certain bodily state of a man or animal, the state, perhaps, which enables the man or animal to enjoy food, sleep and exercise. But we call other things healthy because they are related in various ways to this state. We call a man healthy because he possesses it, pinkness in cheeks healthy because it indicates it, mountain walking healthy because it preserves it, sea voyages healthy because they restore it, an appetite healthy because it results from it, and on on. There is no reason why emotion-words like 'sad' should not be used similarly. What is primarily sad, no doubt, is a certain feeling on the part of a person, but other things may be called sad because they are related to that feeling. A man is sad if he has it; someone's death may be sad if it causes it in the survivors; a sigh may be sad because it indicates or results from it. When, therefore, we are told that a piece of music or moorland is sad, we need not wonder how a feeling can be attributed to a process or tract of earth and rock; our task is not to justify the ascription of a feeling to something which cannot feel, but to say in which of the many possible ways the music or moorland is related to the feeling. For the possibilities are various.

A musical instrument has a sound like a person's voice: indeed, in some languages, like Greek, there is only one word for musical sound and for the human voice. Someone's voice would be called sad if its intonation indicated or resulted from sadness, and musical instruments may be called sad or cheerful if they sound like sad or cheerful voices. A tune which is otherwise neutral may become sad if played on a viola or 'cello instead of a violin.

Again, music could be called sad or triumphant if it caused in the hearer feelings of sadness or triumph.

Again, we saw that to a person in a mood, things appear in an unusual manner; to the depressed man, the decoration of his room, which normally seems clean and bright enough, seems shabby or dark, and so on. A tract of country could be called sad, if it normally looked as normal pieces of country look when you are sad; a piece of music cheerful, if it normally sounds as normal things sound when you are cheerful. How would such an effect be achieved? Perhaps when we are cheerful, we hear certain sounds rather than others which are being made around us, and the music imitates them; or we notice certain movements, or ordinary movements appear brisker and crisper, and the changes in sound provide an analogy.

If a work of art resulted from feelings of sorrow or joy it might be called sorrowful or joyful, but such a work would not, just for that reason, have any special aesthetic merit; it might have merit, however, if it was joyful or sorrowful in some other way, for instance the way just described, or if it moved the hearer or beholder. How, then, can a work of art move us?

Obviously it can move us in the way anything can move us. A barbaric effigy could frighten someone; a cunningly contrived sequence of sounds could be irritating. But there seems to be no aesthetic merit in that. A thing might also excite the pure aesthetic emotion discussed above; in that case it would have aesthetic merit, but hardly by criteria distinct from those discussed under the heading of pure form. Similarly a person who inadvertently makes us laugh has not thereby brought off an aesthetic coup, while a performance by a first-rate clown is probably best judged by criteria of its own.

An artist comes nearer to expressionist success if he moves us by something in a representation; but we must distinguish two ways in which a represented thing can be moving. It may be an object of emotion to people in the represented world. In that case we may say it is represented as moving. A painter represents Iphigenia as pitiable, if he represents her as an object of pity to bystanders at Aulis; Helen is represented as desirable, if she is represented as moving Paris with desire. A picture in which a thing is represented as an object of emotion to people in the picture may be a success by mimetic criteria, but it is not obvious why it should move the beholder.

A thing in a picture can nonetheless be an object of emotion to beholders. A face in a picture can arouse fear or disgust in us; a woman's torso or a bowl of fruit can arouse feelings of desire. That is, if we adhere to the account of emotion given above, we may think of the face as a source of imminent harm to ourselves, think of the pears in the bowl as cool, juicy and sweet for us to eat. Now in fact the face and the pears are not real but represented; they are not, therefore, capable of harming or pleasing us. If, then, they move us, it seems to follow that we are labouring under, and the artist has created, some kind of illusion: for in general to be illuded is to take a semblance for reality. So it would appear to be a sign that the artist has created an illusion if we are moved by things in the picture, and if we are to be moved by things in the picture we must be under an illusion.

Similarly with fiction. A character in a book can be represented as an object of fear, anger, boredom or the like to people in the story, or can arouse such feelings in the reader. When you read a successful horror story, things and events in the story chill your blood; the pornographer endeavours to excite sexual feelings which are directed in the first instance at characters in his story. Since things in stories are unreal, if we have these feelings we must be under an illusion.

Can we say, then, that an artist scores an aesthetic success if he creates an illusion of this sort? Berenson thought so. 'We must come', he says, 'to an agreement as to what, in the art of figure-painting . . . *is* the essential. . . . Painting is an art which aims at giving an abiding impression of artistic reality with only two dimensions. The painter must therefore do consciously what we all do unconsciously—construct his third dimension. And he can accomplish this task only as we accomplish ours, by giving tactile values to retinal impressions. His first business, therefore, is to rouse our tactile sense, for I must have the illusion of being able to touch a figure, I must have the illusion of varying muscular sensations inside my palm and finger corresponding to the various projections of this figure, before I take it for granted as real, and let it affect me lastingly. It follows that the essential in the art of painting—as distinguished from the art of colouring, I beg the reader to observe—is somehow to stimulate our consciousness of tactile values, so that the picture will have at least as much power as the object represented, to appeal to our tactile imagination.' On this showing, a successful picture will be one in which the figures are thought of as objects of touch or feeling to ourselves; and if we do so think of them, and have the sensations in our palms and fingers of which he speaks, we shall probably feel emotions of desire, disgust, and the like—or, perhaps, embarrassment.

This account, however, seems absurd. Pornographic painting and writing, which would succeed by this criterion, are rated very low, and most serious artists would wish to guard against giving beholders emotions towards things in pictures. Horrific stories and paintings have a certain value; but the great masters of horror, among whom we might wish to include, though they excel in other fields too, Aeschylus, Brueghel and Dostoevsky, do more than make us frightened at particular things and happenings in their creations.

I distinguished directed emotions and moods. In general, works of art seem to affect our feelings more by putting us into a mood than by exciting a directed emotion. Even a ghost story rather puts us in a mood of fear than makes us fearful of an individual ghost. If we concentrate on mood, we can understand how a work of art may succeed in the way expressionist theorists have in mind, without invoking illusion.

In the first place, when we are in a mood we notice some things and ignore others. A painter may make clear to us in his picture just the things we would notice if we were in a mood of joy or pity or the like. Indeed, it is clear that this often happens. If you look at a picture by Claude or the young Turner, you are aware of such things in the represented landscape as you would be aware of in a real one, if you were in a mood to enjoy it. In applying, then, the appropriate descriptions to the things in the picture, we are in a mood not perhaps identical with the mood we should experience before the reality, but very similar to it.

Second, we may be brought into a mood by a picture, or, for that matter, by an impressive piece of architecture or natural scenery. In ordinary experience we can be made irritable or depressed by one or two irritating or depressing things; we then get into the way of applying to whatever comes along a description under which it is irritating or depressing. Similarly a piece of luck or good news makes us cheerful. If, then, a painter contrives to make us apply descriptions characteristic of a mood to things in his picture, even if we suffer no illusion and the things in the picture do not move us, we may find it easy to go on and apply similar descriptions to the real things around us. A building which puts us in mind of national glory, or the power of God, or the like, affects our mood in the same way.

That the effect of a representation should extend beyond our contemplation of it, and colour our attitude to other things, is the more readily understandable if it deals with realities or with relationships or situations such as we meet in ordinary life. The Christian may be led by a picture of the Crucifixion to think pious thoughts about God or charitable thoughts about his fellows. The reader of the last book of the *Iliad* may apply Homer's descriptions of Priam to unfortunate old people he meets, and be more easily moved to pity for them. It has been said that Meredith's *The egoist* is salutary reading for young men engaged to be married.

If a work of arts puts us in a mood in any of the ways just sketched, we may say it expresses that mood. Although attempts have been made to find other senses in which a work of art may be expressive of feeling, it is, I think, in this way that we shall do most justice to the insights about feeling mentioned at the beginning of this chapter. A work of art will be a success by expressionist criteria if it expresses or puts us into a mood we should like to be in. On particular occasions we may have reason to wish to be in particular moods, e.g. patriotic, forgiving, devout, and in general we would like to be in a mood in which our eyes are, as we might say, more than usually open to our surroundings, or see deeper than usual into them; in which we find what we see giving us occasion to exercise understanding of how things work; particularly, perhaps, in which it is easy to understand how human beings work, and exercise sympathy. A work of art which leads us to apply rich and intelligent descriptions will be a success in this way.

Can we say that a given work of art expresses one particular feeling or set of feelings? If not, if the way in which it moves us is determined by what we bring to the contemplation of it, then it is implausible to say that works of art are in themselves expressive, for it would be odd if a thing had great power to affect our feelings, but not to affect them in any particular way. In fact, how much we can usefully say about the expressiveness of a work of art depends on the work of art. It is seldom easy to assign any definite effect to a piece of music. Even if a piece of music does move us by imitating the sounds and changes we are aware of when we are in a particular mood, that is difficult to show, because we can seldom say—indeed, it may take a great novelist to say—how our awareness in that mood differs from our awareness at other times. Similarly with patterns, buildings and the like: even though you yourself may value a piece of architecture or design for the emotive effect it has on you, you will probably find it easier to justify your good opinion of it by formalist than by expressionist criteria. Pictures hold an intermediate position. Nobody would say that a Raphael Madonna picture reeks of violence and horror, or praise the gentle tranquillity of a Bosch inferno; but it might be thought that there are many pictures which can have different effects on different beholders, or even on the same beholder at different times; perhaps the same eighteenth-century landscape sometimes seems happy and sometimes tinged with melancholy.

If you say that this Fragonard is a happy picture, and I say that there is something sad about it, the discussion need not break down at that point. We may each say in detail what we see in it; and we will probably find at least that we are applying to the represented landscape descriptions we would apply to a real one in an appreciative mood. Further, although happiness and sadness sound opposed, we are sometimes not sorry to be in a sort of mood which seems poised between the two; if you and I each describe our mood by saying how we are led to think of things in the picture and of other things, it may turn out that our moods are not far apart; at any rate it will appear clearly what in our moods is due to the picture and what to our own past experience, temperaments and so on.

I have now tried to bring out three distinct criteria of aesthetic assessment. I would not wish to claim that there are no others, but these seem to me important. Appeal to one or more of them can be seen in much unphilosophical thought and speech about the things we assess aesthetically; and many disputes in philosophical aesthetics have arisen because writers have taken one of them and tried to make it the sole touchstone of aesthetic merit. That such a course must lead, either to wrong judgements or to absurd defences of right ones, is fairly clear. It is, perhaps, most convenient to illustrate the use of mimetic criteria with representational painting, formalist with music and patterns, and expressionist with literature; but it would be a mistake to take these connections as sacred. In fact, many works of art succeed by criteria of all three kinds. A painting may be a good representation, and moving, and also good as a pattern; a melody may be well suited to the words, and moving, and also good as a change in sound. In particular it is difficult to separate mimetic and expressionist criteria. If an artist is to move us in the ways I have suggested, he must first achieve subtle representational effects; and although in the next chapter I shall talk about expression in the first section and representation in the second, that is not because works of literature can be divided into those that succeed as the one and those that succeed as the other: in general, what succeeds in either way succeeds, and for the same reasons, in both.

5

LITERATURE

1. *Speech and meaning*

Among the things we assess aesthetically, works of literature have a special interest for philosophers. The philosopher is by occupation a dweller among books; he makes, from his own standpoint, a study of language; and there are several philosophical problems connected with literature which do not arise, at least in the same way, over other works of art. For these reasons it is convenient to devote a separate discussion to literature.

We may begin with the question: what exactly is a work of literature? By a work of literature I mean something like the *De corona*, the *Divine comedy*, *Hamlet*. The general view is that these are types, to which particular printed books stand as tokens; in other words, they are related to the books on my shelf as a piece of music is related to performances of it.

There is a certainly a case for holding that *Hamlet* stands in this relation to what we witness at the theatre: we might say that what Shakespeare wrote was something analogous to a musical score, namely a prescription or set of instructions for actors to follow. Even this, however, sounds an incomplete account, since *Hamlet* can be treated and enjoyed in the same way as a novel, epic or sonnet, things which are not enacted or performed;[1] and when we come to novels, epics and sonnets themselves, it becomes most unnatural to say that our shelves contain tokens of these. In ordinary speech the book I take in my hand is said to be, not an instance or example of *Middlemarch*, but a copy of it.

A copy is related to that of which it is a copy, not as a performance to the piece of music performed, but rather as a gramophone record to what is recorded, and what is recorded is of course a performance of a piece of music by a particular player or set of players on a particular occasion. So if a work of literature is that of which you and I have copies, it will be something like a performance; a token, then, rather than a type, even if a paradigmatic token. And that is reasonable. My copy of the *De corona* is a copy of a performance by Demosthenes before the Athenians, and if Demosthenes' speech was a performance, so was Homer's recitation (if we suppose the Homeric poems were originally recited), and so was Jane Austen's writing when she wrote *Emma*. We may say, that those literary works of which we possess copies are original writings or speeches. I shall use the word 'speech' to cover writings as well as vocal deliveries.

Professor C. L. Stevenson[2] claims that works of literature are not types but megatypes. What he means may be explained as follows. We sometimes feel like saying that the words, i.e. the word-types, 'dog' and *chien* are the same word. Instead of saying that, we may say that they stand as tokens to the same megatype. A poem such as the *Odyssey* is strictly (according to Stevenson) a megatype or sequence of megatypes of this sort; so T. W. Allen's Oxford Classical Text and T. E. Lawrence's translation would be tokens of the *Odyssey*, and the *Odyssey* itself would be neither of these, but that of which they are tokens.

The terms 'type' and 'token' were introduced, as we saw, in the interests of a classification of signs. The Stevensonian megatype of which 'dog' and *chien* are tokens can hardly be a sign or word. If anything, it is a thing signified, namely the type of which individual dogs are tokens; for certainly what links 'dog' and *chien* is that they are both words for a dog. Similarly the megatype of *rouge* and 'red' would be the colour red. If the *Odyssey* is to be a megatype, then, it will presumably be the events themselves, the return of Odysseus, fight with the suitors and so on, related in Greek by Homer and in English by Lawrence. I doubt if Stevenson intended to say this, but the idea is worth investigating.

I shall argue below that a large part of the narrative writer's art is skill in selecting and putting together events which will make clear the mental and moral characteristics of the characters concerned; so even if the *Odyssey* is strictly just the sequence of events, it can still be Homer's work and a considerable achievement. It is less plausible, perhaps, to say that lyric poems are megatypes in this sense, but not quite impossible. Take the poem 'Full fathom five':[3] we might give Shakespeare credit for locating Ferdinand's father at the depth of thirty feet; for making his bones coral and his eyes pearls and not the reverse, and so on. Perhaps the suggestion can even be stretched to cover painting. We might say that the megatype of a number of pictures is a young woman holding a child.

When discussing painting, however, I said that an artist has no concept of the scene he is going to paint, apart from his concept of how to represent it, of the pattern he will impose on the canvas. This is even more clearly true of the lyric poet. Shakespeare was going to locate the father at a certain depth *in words*; he was going to metamorphose the bones and eyes in a poem; and his thought of the depth will have been nothing different from his thought of expressions for depth, his thought of what the bones and eyes were to have turned into, nothing different from thought of words like 'coral' and 'pearl'. And the same holds for the epic poet. It is, indeed, possible for a man detained by a nymph on a distant island, to think up expedients for getting home, to consider possible actions and things to use; but when Homer was composing the earlier books of the *Odyssey*, his problem was quite different: he was thinking up possible speeches or things to say. He did not consider alder or poplar as suitable materials to use for a raft, but as suitable materials to say Odysseus used, and their occurrence to him was the occurrence of the words κλήθρη and αἴγειρος.[4] That is, even if composing the *Odyssey* was composing a sequence of events, it was still composing a possible speech, and a possible speech in Greek, the only language in which Homer (let us suppose) could compose speeches. While, then, we may say if we like that the *Odyssey* is strictly the *Odyssey* as it was in Homer's mind, or as he projected it, and hence a type or possibility and not a token or actuality, still it is an ordinary type consisting of Greek type-words, a possibility the fulfilment of which is a speech in Greek, not in just any language. Lawrence's work is not a fulfilment of what Homer planned or conceived, but a translation of a fulfilment of it.

Taking it that works of literature are speeches, we may pass to questions about their meaning and interpretation. What exactly are we enquiring into when we enquire into the meaning of a poem or play? It seems that we want to know, among other things, what a poem expresses, what its emotional content is; but how can that be ascertained? Can we discover the emotive meaning of a poem only by feeling it, or may we use evidence and argument? If the latter, what evidence may we use, and what is a good argument? Should we, as some writers hold, confine ourselves to internal evidence, to what can be gathered simply from the text, and adopt that interpretation according to which the work of literature has most aesthetic merit or is most satisfying? Or is the distinction between internal and external evidence impossible to sustain, and should we use biographical material about the author and aim at an interpretation which will make clear his intentions in writing? These questions concern more than the technique of criticism, for if we can say how the emotive meaning of a poem can be established, it will be clear how a poem can *have* emotive meaning and be expressive.

Professor P. F. Strawson in his well-known article 'On referring'[5] distinguished the meaning of a sentence from its use. To enquire into the meaning of a sentence is to enquire into the general rules for its use. Affirmative sentences are used to make statements, and to enquire into the use of such a sentence by a particular speaker on a particular occasion is to ask what statement he used it to make, i.e. to what thing or things he referred and what he said about them. Different sentences (e.g. 'I am bald', 'Frederick is bald') may be used to state the same fact, and the same sentence, e.g. 'I am bald', may be used to state different facts. And we can understand the meaning of a sentence we see written up, e.g. 'I love Mabel', without knowing to what persons the writer was referring, or, consequently, what statement he was making.

Strawson's account is helpful, but needs adaptation. It is not quite natural to say we use sentences to make statements. Rather, on occasions when a person would be said to use a sentence, he uses it for any purpose except that of making a statement. I have just used 'I love Mabel' to illustrate Strawson's account. Similarly interrogative sentences are not used to ask questions or elicit information; 'Where is the pen of my aunt?' is used to make fun of teaching French. To make statements we use words, that is, utter them, string them together in sentences according to grammatical rules; and to understand the meaning of a sentence is to know the words and construction. Knowing a word is knowing how it is pronounced or written, and also how it is used or what can be said by using it.

We may explain this last requirement by introducing the notion of a speech act. J. L. Austin tried to distinguish certain acts of speaking from acts which we perform in or by speaking.[6] His actual findings have been disputed, but there do seem to be certain acts, which might fairly be called acts of speaking, because they can be performed only in languages, and learning a language is learning how to perform them. Learning Latin or French is learning how to assert or deny things, order or forbid things, and ask questions, in those languages. You can ask a question in French, for instance, by prefacing an assertion with 'Est-ce que c'est que'. So assertions, denials, questions, orders and prohibitions may be called speech acts.[7] To understand their character we may compare them with legal acts, like marrying someone or making a will, which we perform by and only by following procedures established in the laws or customs of particular societies; or with acts like castling, bidding two no trumps, which we perform by following procedures laid down in the laws of a game. A man bids two no trumps in bridge, in accordance with the laws of bridge, and bidding no trumps is nothing outside a game of bridge; he makes a will in France in accordance with the laws of France, and will-making is nothing outside a politically organised society; and he asserts something in French, in accordance with the laws of French, and asserting is nothing outside a language.

Knowing how a word is used is knowing what difference the use of it would or could make to a speech act, and we may teach words by explaining what speech acts a person using them performs—the word 'mainbrace', for instance, by explaining what order a man gives when he says 'Splice the mainbrace'. If, then, we know the words and constructions used in a speech, we know what speech act the speaker is or could be performing. We may call this knowing the meaning of the words. This is the level mentioned in Chapter 1 at which anyone knowing the language in which a poem is written must be able to understand the poem: he must know the meaning of the words. And what I call the meaning of the words is what Strawson calls the meaning of the sentence.

Besides the meaning of the words of a speech, we may enquire into the meaning of the speech act, the assertion, question or whatever it may be. The difference between the two sorts of enquiry is easily illustrated. Suppose we are talking about Shelley and you say 'He's not a very meaty poet': if I am puzzled by your speech, it is probably because I do not know what you mean, in this context, by 'meaty'; what are you denying when you deny that a poet is meaty? Suppose, on the other hand, that you are standing on a railway platform in the rush-hour, and I force my way through the crowd, say in significant tones 'It's raining again' and withdraw before you have time to reply: you understand the meaning of my words, know well what I am asserting, but may wonder, even if it is indeed raining, and still more if it is not, what could be the meaning of my assertion. 'Why did he assert that it is raining again?', you ask yourself; 'What did he mean by it?'

To ask the meaning of a speech act, is to ask what the speaker means or might mean to achieve by performing it. The range of possible answers is extremely wide. Suppose I say to you 'That dog Richards got from Cumberland is a remarkably good one': I may

E

be trying to distract your mind from a gloomy topic; make you jealous of Richards or sorry that your sporting days are over; induce you to improve the quality of your own kennel; or simply keep the conversation alive. Among the possible aims of a speech is to affect someone emotionally. It is clearly this possibility which is of special interest to the aesthetician, but before we come to it, we should get clearer the general notion of the meaning of a speech act.

We do not have to know what a person is saying to know the meaning of his speech. If I say to you 'Have you never learned to practise aposiopesis?' you may not know what it is I am asking you if you have learned to practise, but you may know that I am trying to be funny or offensive. Further, knowledge of a language guarantees only that we know what speech acts speakers might be performing; often language is ambiguous, and we decide which of several speech acts a speaker is in fact performing by considering why he is saying what he says. Thus take the sonnet beginning 'When in the chronicles of wasted time I see descriptions of the fairest wights':[8] 'wasted' could mean misspent, or simply past; we decide it means the latter, because then the whole assertion will be more likely to gratify the person Shakespeare is addressing, and that, we think, is what he means to do. The question, then, what a speech act means, is separate from, and though usually not invariably posterior to the question what the words mean.

It is also separate from the question to what the speaker is referring. If I accost a stranger and say 'In two days you will see a badger' he knows what I am saying and to whom I am referring—himself—but not what I mean. And if I say to you 'The high priest of English literature is coming to dinner' you may understand my words and also the meaning of my assertion—I mean to mystify you—but not know to whom I am referring. Nevertheless, knowing the reference of a speech helps us to understand the speaker's meaning in making it. If I say 'Your father has a face like Augustus' whether you think I am trying to conciliate you depends on whether you think I am referring to the Roman emperor or to a Pekinese, known to us both, of the same name.

I said a moment ago that the meaning of a speech-act can be to affect someone's feelings; we must now consider when this is so. Our first inclination might be to say that a speech act is meant to excite or calm a given feeling, when and only when that is the intention of the speaker. A person, however, can intend to bring something about only when he has means of doing so—you cannot intend, but only hope, to win a lottery—and we would not say that he intended to achieve a particular end if he adopted none of the means to it, but did only what was likely to prevent its realisation. What, then, are the means open to a speaker who wishes to move someone? Tones of voice, references and allusions, and also words, constructions, figures of speech. Suppose someone addresses you before company in an aggressive manner: you can still believe that he means to make you calm and cheerful if the words he utters are 'You're the best friend I have and the finest man I know', but not if they are 'You're a liar and a conceited fool'. Here the speech itself seems to have a certain aptitude to produce an emotive effect. Let us see more precisely how this is possible.

Besides its meaning, a word may have an aptitude to move emotionally which I shall call its emotive force. A distinction between the two is often attempted by moral philosophers who wish to contrast the meaning of the word 'good' with its force, but they do not always draw it correctly.[4] To give the meaning of a word is to say what a person using it thereby says; and two words in different languages, e.g. 'good' and ἀγαθός, have the same meaning if people using them thereby say the same thing. To give the force of a word is to say what aptitude it has to move emotionally. The force of a word depends on such features as its length, its sound, whether it is formal or colloquial, archaic or new-coined. Hence there is no presumption that words with the same meaning will have the same force, e.g. that what is said about the force of the monosyllable 'good' will be true of the force of the trisyllable ἀγαθός. Further, while we can give a general account of the meaning of a word, we cannot give any general account of its force. A word has a force only in a context, and the same word, because of the same features, its length and so on, can have a different force in different contexts. Hence it is useless to ask what is *the* force of any word, e.g. 'abandon'; we can say only that in one case, e.g. 'He was abandoned by all his friends', its force is to excite pity, and another, e.g. Dr Johnson's 'A man might write such stuff for ever if he would abandon his mind to it', contempt. Contrary to the belief of many moral philosophers, this is particularly true of the word 'good'. Consider: 'He was a good friend to me', 'I'd like him better if he were not so very good', 'He's the sort of man who is very interested in good food', 'His work is better but still not good'. They seem to think only of the shop-assistant's soupy 'This is a very good line, madam'.

Force attaches also to syntactical constructions. The construction 'if not p then not q' has the same meaning as the construction 'p or not q' inasmuch as a person using either says the same thing. Still there is, I think, a difference in compelling or minatory force, such as a blackmailer would appreciate, between 'If you do not pay me two thousand pounds, there will be no wedding on the 24th' and 'You will pay me two thousand pounds or there will be no wedding on the 24th'. Similarly with such figures of speech as zeugma and aposipesis. Zeugma does not affect the meaning of the words: you make the same assertion whether you say 'She went home weeping in a sedan chair' or 'She went home in tears and a sedan chair'; but in the latter case you check any feelings of pity which may have been rising in us.

How are such effects achieved? Words and speeches are gestures or movements on the part of the speaker. Archaic words, then, and quaint constructions, like archaic clothes or quaint manners, can have the effect of making the speaker seem archaic or quaint, and some authors use them with this aim directly in view: so at times Beerbohm, who plays the buffoon *in propria persona* for us. But often and naturally enough attributes of the speech are transferred to the things spoken of. Obvious examples are onomatopoeic effects, e.g. Milton's 'Their lean and flashy songs grate on their scrannel pipes of wretched straw'. For a more subtle example we could take the last words of Browne's *Urn Burial*: 'As content with six foot as the Moles of Adrianus', where the contrasted simplicity and magnificence of the expressions 'six foot' and 'the Moles of Adrianus' are transferred to the graves.

Again, we saw that a painter can move the beholder if the beholder is induced to apply certain descriptions to the things in the picture. A writer can give his work expressive force by employing the appropriate descriptions himself. If the reader accepts them and applies them to the things written of—and unless they are grotesque he probably will, since that is the line of least resistance—he is moved. Simile and metaphor are emotive devices of this sort. 'Like to the race of leaves is that of men. The wind sheds the leaves onto the ground, and the flourishing wood grows more when the season of spring comes round; and so does the race of men now grow, now fail.'[10] Homer does not move us merely by his words and word order, or his lines would not survive translation: he tells us that a description of leaves, which he supplies and which is itself typical of a mood of gentle, meditative sadness, is applicable to men. And even without direct metaphor or simile an author can select phrases which, by virtue of the meanings of the words in them, have a definite force. We have no regular word for a squiggly shape; the phrases 'the shape of a river', however, and 'the shape of a snake' (or, what are similar, 'undulating' and 'serpentine') can be used to say that something, e.g. a queue of men, has a squiggly shape, and the force of the speech will be different depending on which we use, because different feelings are excited by rivers (or waves) and snakes. Or again, there is a regular word for a round shape, namely 'round'. Instead of using it, however, a writer might say 'His face was the shape of the full moon' or 'His face was the shape of a haddock's eye'. The former expression might be preferable if he wanted us to feel that the face was venerable or sublime, the latter if he wanted it to seem repellant.

We should observe that in these cases the force is determined by the meanings of the words used, and is therefore a matter for rational argument. It is not the case that we merely 'feel' the difference in force between 'His face was the shape of the full moon' and 'His face was the shape of a haddock's eye'. 'The full moon' is an expression for the full moon; 'a haddock's eye' is an expression for a haddock's eye; and we can claim that the second speech is more apt than the first to excite feelings of revulsion or horror, on the ground that a haddock's eye is more likely to excite such feelings than the full moon. Anyone who wants to dispute this interpretation and say that 'His face was the shape of a haddock's eye' is apt to move the reader differently, must argue that a haddock's eye, either in itself or to anyone who has read what precedes our sentence, would be an object of different feelings, e.g. pitiful rather than ghastly. Hence on the one hand we may agree with Mr J. Benson[11] that it is wrong to deny 'that the expression of emotion is ever brought about by means of the conceptual function of language'—wrong, that is, to make a complete divorce between thinking and feeling in the interpretation of literature. But on the other we should observe that the difference in meaning of the expressions 'a haddock's eye', 'the full moon', makes a difference to the force only, and not to the meaning, of the whole phrases 'the shape of a haddock's eye', 'the shape of the full moon'. A person who says 'His face was the shape of the full moon' is not saying 'His face was the shape of the full moon, whatever that may be' (contrast: 'A chameleon is the colour of its background'), but rather: 'You know the shape of the full moon: well, his face was that shape.' And hence he makes the same assertion as the person who says: 'His face was the shape of a haddock's eye.'

It thus appears that the words of a speech have, independently of the speaker's intentions and even of their reference, a certain aptitude to move emotionally. The thesis (commonly associated with Professors W. K. Wimsatt and Monroe T. Beardsley[12]) that the critic who wishes to establish the meaning of a poem for purposes of aesthetic appreciation and assessment, should make use only of internal evidence or stick to what is written on the page, this may first be understood as the thesis that the meaning which is of aesthetic importance is, not indeed the meaning of the words, but the emotive meaning of the speech-acts precisely insofar as this is determined or indicated by the words in the ways we have just been considering. What should we say about this? One objection is that before we can start using internal evidence, we must locate or identify the work of literature it is internal to, pick out our poem, as it might be, from the rest of what is written on the page, the page number, printer's marks and so on; and we identify as our text what the author intended us to take as the text, thus already using external evidence.[13] This must, I think, be admitted. We could, of course, say that we see poems in books in the way we see faces in clouds, but that sounds implausible. Still, Wimsatt and Beardsley might maintain that once we have identified our poem we should argue for our interpretation only from internal evidence. A more damaging objection is that the whole distinction between internal and external evidence is misconceived.[14] It is impossible to understand any speech without knowing a certain amount about the world—our knowledge of the meaning of words is not independent of our knowledge of the things they are words for. And it is impossible to set boundaries to the knowledge which affects the emotive force of a given poem; it certainly includes what we know of the author and the things he is referring to. Thus (to take a simple example) though Catullus' poem *Ille mi par esse deo videtur* is a translation of Sappho's φαίνεταί μοι κῆνος 'ίσος θέοισιν, they derive a difference in force from the fact that the reference of 'mi' is a man, and the reference of μοῖ a woman.[15] (And the English translation of this line 'Him rival to the gods I place' may affect us differently depending on whether or not we know that the writer is Mr Gladstone.)

I think we may allow validity to this objection while still retaining part of the Wimsatt–Beardsley thesis. A poem's aesthetic merit, at least by expressionist criteria, certainly seems to lie simply in the aptitude of its words to move the reader in ways like those we have surveyed. But how the reader is disposed to be affected depends on his knowledge of the author, the author's intentions and allusions, and the world generally—all matters on which he will naturally try to inform himself so far as he can—so that the aesthetic merit of the poem lies in its ability to affect people with this knowledge; and it is senseless to enquire into the emotive force of a poem without considering for whom, and in the light of what knowledge or beliefs. We might say that the dispute arose because Wimsatt and Beardsley concentrated on the objects of the reader's feelings and their critics on the causes; and both are in fact relevant.

As an illustration of what has been said, take the lines:

> That time of year thou mayst in me behold
> When yellow leaves, or none, or few, do hang
> Upon those boughs which shake against the cold,
> Bare ruined choirs, where late the sweet birds sang.[16]

A question might arise about the meaning of the word 'choirs': does it mean sets of singers or places where people sing? We think the latter, because to say that the branches are bare ruined sets of singers would be mystifying and frigid—we decide the meaning of the word by considerations about the meaning of the speech.

What is the emotive meaning of the lines? It seems impossible to maintain that they are apt to excite a mood of cheerful joviality, or even one of quiet hope. The author is inviting us to think of him as like a time of year which, drawing on our knowledge of the Northern hemisphere, we may identify as November. Now it is certainly possible to think of November under jovial descriptions— as a good time for pears and apples, a time when we can draw the curtains after tea and sit round a blazing fire—or under descriptions expressive of hope—as a time when next year's buds become visible. Shakespeare, however, has chosen descriptions different in force. He has adverted to sapless falling leaves—something sad; to the departure (with no mention of their probable return) of agreeable birds—a matter for regret; to cold, which is unpleasant, particularly when you cannot stand firm, but shake against it. To think of November in the way suggested is to feel melancholy, and a person who resembles November at the points indicated is an object of sympathetic pity.

So far the interpretation of the poem is a matter, not for subjective feeling, but for easy demonstration; but the question has been raised whether the fourth line contains an allusion to ruined monasteries. As we may know that next year's buds appear in England in November, so we may know that blackened monastic ruins were a common sight in England when Shakespeare wrote, and passers-by would have heard tell of, even if they did not remember, the monks and their singing. If Shakespeare is indeed alluding to this, the poem contains an admixture of bitterness, for a person who thinks of ruined monasteries and is prepared to compare the monks to sweet

birds must feel slightly bitter. Or, if he would rather compare them
to vultures, and considers the dissolution of the monasteries socially
beneficial, he will be out of sympathy, and the effect of the line for
him will be entirely spoilt. What, then is the effect of the line? The
mere realisation that Shakespeare might be alluding to ruined
monasteries has changed our ability to be moved by it. If it can be
shown that he was not, we may be able to appreciate the poem as
we would if the question had never arisen. If it were shown that
Shakespeare was alluding to ruined monasteries, we would say that
the poem has a touch of bitterness, not on the ground that Shakespeare felt bitter, but on the ground that that is how it would make a
reader with our knowledge feel, if it were not spoilt for him. Similar
points may be made about the reference of the word 'thou'.

On the present showing, our chief ground for saying that a work of
literature expresses a given feeling will be that the descriptions in
it are such that to consider them applicable is to have that feeling.
Thoughts characteristic of that feeling are expressed or put into
words in it. Many expressionist aestheticians have given a different
account. Collingwood, for instance, holds that a poem is an expression of feeling in the way in which swearing is an expression of anger:
the poet's consciousness of his total sensual and emotional experience
erupts in the words of his poem. This seems altogether too romantic.
Some poets take a long time over their compositions, correcting,
revising, polishing. Horace in his *Ars poetica* maintains that only so
can good poetry be written. What, then, was Horace doing in the
years[17] when his poem 'Fountain of Bandusia' was maturing?
According to Collingwood his occupation was 'to discover emotions
in himself of which he was unaware, and by permitting the audience
to witness the discovery, enable them to make a similar discovery
about themselves'.[18] But would Horace's emotions have stayed
constant so long to be explored? And further, even if we grant that to
compose poetry we must dominate our emotions with consciousness,
is exploring them the right way to set about it? The normal way of
dominating a feeling is to think not about the feeling but about its
objects. Thus if you wish to dominate your dislike of someone, you
will do your best to think about him, ask yourself whether he is really
a threat to your interests, whether he can help being as he is,[19] and
so on. And if to feel an emotion is to think of objects in a certain way,
to become conscious of your emotion is to think how you would
describe them.[20]

Horace, I suggest, spent the time before publishing the *Odes* in
thinking about the fountain of Bandusia: not so much feeling

emotions and exploring them, as exploring the aptitude of the fountain of Bandusia to excite emotion, thinking out descriptions relating it to objects of rational pursuit and avoidance. This inevitably takes time. Things move us only when thought of in a certain way, and the things about which poets write move us under descriptions which would naturally occur to someone only over a long period of reflection. You could hardly, as you hurtle past it on the *autostrada*, be conscious of the fountain of Bandusia under the description 'provides coolness for tired oxen and wandering cattle'.[21] It is because the reader of a lyric poem gets the fruits of hours of laborious thought crowded into a few seconds, that it makes such an unusual impact on him.

If we accept this account, a moving poem might be written in cold blood, though when a poet contemplates his finished work he may, if he is not exhausted, feel what his readers feel. If we accept Collingwood's account, contrary to his intention it will normally be impossible for the feeling which inspired the poet to be communicated to the reader. The feeling of the reader can only be that involved in thinking of the things spoken of under the descriptions offered, and that feeling will seldom if ever be one to move us to write poetry.

> Tir'd with all these, for restful death I cry,
> As to behold desert a beggar born,
> And needy nothing trimm'd in jollity,
> And purest faith unhappily forsworn,
> And gilded honour shamefully misplac'd . . . [22]

If we really think of the world under these descriptions, then, as Shakespeare says, we cry for restful death, not for paper and pen.

2. *Description and narrative*

The drift of the last section was that expressionist criteria can be applied to works of literature in much the way in which they can be applied to pictures, and it is natural to suppose that the same holds for mimetic criteria. After all, we often say that a writer gave a vivid picture of life on the Upper Zambesi, or completely misrepresented the state of things in Ireland, or executed a full-length verbal portrait of his grandfather. But before we see how mimetic criteria apply to literature, we ought to consider just how close the analogy between a speech and a picture is.

Hume[23] seems to have thought that a speech is exactly like a picture; at least, he thought that the belief that Caesar died in his bed is a vivid mental picture of Caesar dying in his bed, and the belief that Caesar did not die in his bed a blurred or flickering picture of the same scene: the speeches 'Caesar died in his bed' and 'Caesar did not die in his bed' could then easily be explained as verbal copies or translations of these pictures. This will not do at all. There seem to be no such mental pictures as Hume invokes, and anyhow the difference between asserting, denying, asking, ordering and forbidding cannot be explained in terms of degrees of vividness.

Plato[24] suggested that names are just like pictures, and an affirmative speech is like applying a picture to a thing—the speech 'You are a man' is like giving a picture of a man to the person before you and (as Plato was shrewd enough to recognise) saying 'This is your picture'. Those[25] who favour an analysis in terms of phrastic and neustic are taking the same line. The phrastic is a sort of picture of a scene, e.g. of your shutting the door, and the neustic is the application of this, 'It is so' or 'Is it so?' or 'Let it be so'. And the same may be said of Russell's theory of descriptions.[26] Russell analysed the speech 'The present king of France is bald' as 'There is one thing and one only such that it is now king of France and bald'. Here the first part is a sort of neustic: 'Is the king of France bald?' could be analysed 'Is there one thing and one only such that . . . ?'; and speech generally is made a matter of asserting that a structure of objects of immediate awareness (a Russellian description was intended to have such a structure as its meaning) corresponds to reality—or asking whether it does, or ordering that it should, or the like.

All these analyses fail in the same way: the analysandum appears unanalysed in the analysis. If we want to know what speech is like, we want to know what asserting, asking, and other such speech-acts are like, and it is no use telling us that asserting is like asserting that a picture represents reality, and asking like asking whether it does. In the phrastic-neustic account the whole of the speech is contained in the neustic 'It is so' or 'Is it so?', and the phrastic, precisely because it could be replaced by a picture, is not part of what we are trying to analyse.

Some account of speech acts has already been given: they are acts performed in a language by compliance with grammatical rules. For the rest, they are not accompaniments of or operations on representation, but analogues of it. A speaker does not draw a picture and assert or deny that it reflects reality; he asserts or denies instead of depicting. As we may say what is represented in a picture, so we may say what is asserted, denied or asked in a speech; and as the artist tries, by using principles and techniques of painting such as were described in Chapter 3, to make clear what is the case in his picture, so, as I shall say more fully below, the writer tries, by using his knowledge of the language and various literary techniques, to make clear what is asserted, denied, and in general said in his speech.

The Russellian analysis is open to criticism on another count: it does not do justice to the referential function of words in ordinary speeches. If we are to state a fact about the world, it is not enough to say that there is something which uniquely satisfies a description but we have to provide means of identifying this thing, locating it in the world. To do this we must refer, or be able to refer, at least to some thing or event which will serve as a reference point. In Russell's example, the meaning of the words 'the present king of France' is exploited to secure reference, not to say something about something: the speech-act is the assertion that the present king of France is bald, not the assertion that something is now (the word 'now' in fact contains a covert reference to the speaker and to the things by which the speaker orientates himself in space and time) king of France and bald. But although Russell's analysis is thus inappropriate to *bona fide* speeches, it is appropriate to, and thus gives us a way of distinguishing, fiction. A novel, or at least a fairy tale, could begin in just the recommended manner: 'There was one man and only one who was king of Ruritania and he had a beautiful wife' etc. We might say that the language of fiction differs from *bona fide* speech in that the referential function of the words is suppressed.

But not completely. Ryle in an early article[27] turned the full force of the theory of descriptions on *Pickwick Papers*, and reached the opinion that 'at the end of the book the pseudo-proper name 'Mr Pickwick' professes to designate someone to whom occurred all the events which the book as a whole purports to record.' That is, the sentence 'Mr Pickwick is somewhat infirm now' should be analysed: 'There was one man and only one who was called Samuel Pickwick Esq, and who (here insert the text of Dickens' novel) . . . and who is now quite infirm'. This can hardly be right. If it were, then in a *bona fide* biography of Queen Victoria, the genuine proper name 'Queen Victoria' ought to end by designating someone to whom occurred all the events related in the book. Now suppose that half way through the biographer makes a slip and asserts that the queen went to the Isle of Wight in January 1857, when in fact she did not. It would seem to follow that from then on the book is pure fiction; for 'Queen Victoria' professes to designate someone who was married to Prince Albert and went to the Isle of Wight in January 1857, and there is no such person. If to avoid this consequence we say that 'Queen Victoria' designates a person identifiable by a limited number of characteristics, such as that of being queen of England for the second half of the nineteenth century, we can say the same of 'Mr Pickwick': it refers to a person identifiable by a limited number of characteristics, such as the presidency of the Pickwick Club. And that being so, even if the novel considered as a single protracted speech is not referential, the use of particular words may be referential in a way: they may be used to refer, not indeed to things in the real world, but to things in the world of the book, locatable in the represented space and time.

In the same article Ryle tried to explain fiction as a kind of pretending. His favoured expression is that 'Dickens' propositions . . . pretend to be true of a Mr Pickwick'. I do not think that a proposition is capable of pretence. Dickens was, but it is hard to say definitely what he was pretending to do or be when he wrote *Pickwick*. Pretending to write about an inhabitant of nineteenth-century England? It would be more natural to say that, if he announced an intention of doing a life of William IV, strewed materials for such a biography around his study, and then under cover of them read *Humphry Clinker*. Pretending to be a biographer? There are various ways of doing that, but writing a novel like *Pickwick* is hardly one of them. Perhaps Rolfe when he wrote *Don Tarquinio* pretended he was editing and translating an autobiographical document, but the pretence occurred less in the body of the work than in the preliminaries. Could Dickens have been pretending if, as seems likely, he did not think he was pretending. We normally speak of pretence where there is an attempt to deceive or dissimulate; it seems as out of place to say that Dickens was pretending, as to say that a painter pretends when he paints a fictitious scene.

Ryle elsewhere[28] suggests that acting is a kind of pretending. That too is implausible. Suppose Richard Burton and Elizabeth Taylor play the parts of Othello and Desdemona. Does Mr Burton pretend that he is a mercenary of moorish extraction in the service of the republic of Venice? He cannot expect us to believe that. Does he pretend to murder Miss Taylor? If the audience thinks that Miss Taylor is being murdered there will be a stampede. Does he then pretend to murder Desdemona? But Desdemona *is* murdered: there is no pretence about her death as there is, at one time, about Juliet's. That fact is that Mr Burton and Miss Taylor *represent* (perhaps by *imitating* the movements of an ill-assorted couple) a series of events culminating in a murder; and Dickens' relating of a series of events in words referring to things locatable in his assertions, is more akin to representation than to anything else.

If a speech is analogous and similar to a picture, that suggests, as I said above, that it succeeds by mimetic criteria if it is clear what is asserted, asked and so on in it. In fact, some writing which we call good does seem to be good for just this reason. Thus if a piece of philosophy is good as philosophy, and also has aesthetic merit, is a pleasure to read, that is probably because the author has made clear questions he is asking and what answers he is giving. Again, we have seen that a speaker may try to move his hearers to some course of action or inaction, that is, get them to do something by exciting or quieting an emotion. He may also try to persuade them, that is, get them to do something by giving a reason for doing it. If he adopts the latter course, his primary aim must be clarity, and a speech can be an aesthetic success because in it reasons for doing things are exhibited with striking clearness and economy. If literary merit is claimed for some of the speeches in Thucydides, for instance that of Diodotus on Mytilene,[29] it would probably be on these grounds; and the difference in character between Demosthenes' Philippic orations and Cicero's might be held to lie in this, that Demosthenes seeks chiefly to give reasons, while Cicero seeks chiefly to stir up feelings.

How can an author make clear what he is saying? In the first place, by an accurate selection of words and construction of sentences, since as we have seen, what is said depends directly on what words are used in what constructions. When we call a work of philosophy or history ill-written, it is usually on the ground that the author has failed here,[30] and the successful wit, even the successful humourist, is distinguished for felicity at this level. It should, of course, be recognised that although clarity has to do with the meaning of words, and is the mark of knowing a language, when we consider whether a speech is good because clear we do not consider only the meaning of the words to the exclusion of their force. The expressions used must not have an aptitude to arouse feelings which would obscure the hearer's or reader's judgement, but rather an aptitude to make it easy to weigh what is said unemotionally.

But though a writer needs a mastery of his language sufficient to ensure that it is clear at any juncture what he is saying, this alone will not make his novel or play a mimetic success. (The same holds, indeed, for a history, or for a speech embodying an extended argument, like a philosophical essay or a political oration.) He shows his artistry even more in devising, selecting and deploying his material.

That is because a novelist relates (and actors enact) a sequence of events or story, and if the work is to succeed, the story must be followed. The following of processes and changes generally was discussed in Chapter 2,[31] and I suggested that to follow a change you must be able to say what is going on at any moment, and ideally in such terms that your account renders the successive developments intelligible. The same holds for following a story which is being related or enacted. At the least you should be able to say where the various characters are and how things are with them at any juncture. Suppose a judge interrupts the examination of a witness and says: 'Just a minute. Why did the witness, if he saw the accused threaten the barmaid with a revolver, not try to summon the police?' If counsel replies: 'With submission, m'lud, the witness has stated that he was already lying bound and gagged under a table' we nudge each other and whisper 'The judge has not been following the story'. But, as I say, the reader's understanding of how things are with the characters should be sufficiently deep to render their actions intelligible. When Elizabeth Bennet runs into Mr Darcy at Pemberley, she is much agitated and confused. That is intelligible if she is coming to regret having refused him but does not wish to seem to be pursuing him. It is not so intelligible if she is coming to repent of having refused Mr Collins, and to see things through his eyes; and a person who thinks that that is how things are with her is scarcely following the story.

Now it might be thought that an author has simply to say, in good English or whatever his language may be, that his character has certain characteristics or long-term aims, and all will be pellucid. But in fact his task is more difficult. A novelist can say that a character has a certain readily perceptible characteristic, like blue eyes, and the reader must take his word: it is clear that the character is blue-eyed. Similarly the novelist can say that a character did or underwent whatever he, the novelist, pleases, and although the reader may grumble, he cannot withold belief. If Dickens had written: 'Then Mr Pickwick slipped some arsenic into Mr Wardle's punch' we should be disgusted, but we could not say 'Mr Pickwick does not poison old Wardle's punch in *Pickwick Papers*'. But when an author attributes a mental or moral characteristic to someone in his book we may, I think, suspend belief and come in the end to reject his statement. Even if Dickens had written 'Mr Pickwick was grasping, vindictive and sly' we could still say 'Mr Pickwick is not grasping, vindictive or sly; Dickens may have thought he was, but it is clear from *Pickwick Papers* that Mr Pickwick is generous, forgiving and open'.

The reason is that the question whether a person is intelligent or foolish, vengeful or forgiving, open or sly, is not independent of the question what he does. In real life we attribute mental and moral characteristics to a person on the basis of his words and actions, and if a writer is to make it clear that someone has a given mental or moral characteristic, he must do it by the actions, words and thoughts he attributes to him. He must, therefore, think up the right actions and put them together in the right way. And since it is the mental and moral qualities of the characters which provide the key to developments in the story, it is by his choice of narrative material that the author makes his work a mimetic success.

The same holds for plays. It is not enough to give Electra the words 'I am not really very fond of my mother': the dramatist must make her show this in other ways if we are to swallow the matricide. As Aristotle, who set a high value on mimetic criteria, observed, the story or plot is the soul of the tragedy.[32] And similarly with much writing that is not fictional. The biographer sets out to relate a series of actions and happenings. Many historians are historians of processes, of wars or of the rise or fall of states or institutions. Their works succeed if the processes can be followed, and we follow insofar as the characters of the people and institutions become clear to us. Even when a historian aims simply at describing a state of affairs, as it might be the state of England at the accession of George III, he reveals how things were then, not just by reciting the laws of the day, but by selecting and relating illustrative events.

There is this difference, that in a history, developments are understandable and acceptable if they can be explained somehow or other. We understand a death if something caused it, however sudden or unforseen it may be. We understand a man doing something if there was some reason or motive for doing it, even if it is not a reason or motive we would have expected to weigh with him. In fiction we call for more consistence in people's actions, and do not even like anything serious to befall them, unless it is the sort of thing which would naturally happen to a person of such a character. The historian is limited by what actually occurred, and must manoeuvre his events and explanations to fit each other. He may be praised for discovering and selecting the former, but he shows his inventiveness in the latter. The writer of fiction, on the other hand, not only selects and arranges but invents his episodes; it is only if he has let his story get out of hand that he needs to invent explanations, and even the discovery of explanations is ideally left as much as possible to the reader.

These remarks must conclude our survey of problems connected with literature. It has, of course, been only a survey, and incomplete at that: the reader will have found that many questions which interest him have been touched on too lightly or not at all. The same holds, indeed, for the earlier chapters of this book. Throughout I have had to be selective, and in selecting I have particularly favoured topics of current or recent philosophical debate, my idea being that these will provide the easiest entry into aesthetics for students of philosophy. For the rest, an introduction should introduce its subject, not exhaust it, and a philosophical introduction should not aim at disposing of all the interesting philosophical problems and leaving only hackwork to be done. I shall be amply content with what I have written, if the reader has received the impression that the field of aesthetics is one which offers exciting opportunities for the daring and resolute prospector.

NOTES AND BIBLIOGRAPHY

CHAPTER 1

1. Clive Bell: *Art*, ch. 1.

2. So S. Hampshire: 'Logic and appreciation' in *World Review*, 1952. (This, with some other works mentioned below, is reprinted in *Aesthetics and Language*, Ed. W. Elton.)

3. So V. Aldrich: *Philosophy of art*, ch. 1.

4. F. Sibley: 'Aesthetic concepts' in *Philosophical Review*, 1959; 'Objectivity and aesthetics' in *Aristotelian Society Proceedings*, suppl. vol. 1968; 'Colours' in *Aristotelian Society Proceedings*, 1967–8.

5. For the transcendental mechanics of aesthetic judgement, see *Critique of judgement*, ss. 35 ff.

6. See, for instance, J. O. Urmson: 'What makes a situation aesthetic' in *Aristotelian Society Proceedings*, suppl. vol. 1954; W. E. Kennick: 'Does traditional aesthetics rest on a mistake?' in *Mind*, 1958. (This, with some other works mentioned below, is reprinted in *Collected papers on aesthetics*, Ed. C. Barrett.) Most modern writers would reject any attempt to set up a single criterion by which things are to be judged aesthetically, but there is not such general agreement that aesthetic thinking is not all of one single type, to be recognised by formal peculiarities.

7. My summary is based on Wittgenstein's own statements (see especially *Philosophical investigations*, I, ss. 66–7; *Brown book*, I, s. 17) which contain the seeds of several slightly different interpretations. Some of his followers emphasise the idea of having a reasonable number of a set of characteristics (so R. Bambrough in 'Universals and family resemblances' in *Aristotelian Society Proceedings*, 1960–1 and, most conspicuously, C. L. Stevenson in 'On "What is a poem" ' *in Philo-*

sophical Review, 1957); others the rope simile and the idea of connecting chains (so A. R. Manser in 'Games and family resemblances' in *Philosophy*, 1967.)

8. So R. Wollheim: *Art and its objects*, s. 42.

9. See Plato: *Sophist*, 240 a–c. Among recent works which bring out the difficulty and offer accounts I saw too late to discuss in Chapter 3 are: R. Squires: 'Depicting' in *Philosophy*, 1969; N. Goodman, *Languages of art*, Chapter 1.

10. A temptation to bait the critics has haunted philosophy from its beginnings. In Plato's *Ion* a prominent Homeric critic is asked why we should listen to him on the *Iliad* rather than to, say, a general. There is nothing described by Homer which does not seem to fall within some specialised field.

11. This opinion is opposed by J. A. Passmore 'The dreariness of aesthetics' in *Mind*, 1951. He does not, however, trace it to what I take to be its roots.

12. Locke: *Essay*, II, xx, 1.

13. Locke: *Essay*, II, vii, 3.

14. Hume: *Treatise*, I, iii, 14, Ed. Selby-Bigge, p. 172.

15. Hume: *Treatise*, III, i, 2, Ed. Selby-Bigge, p. 472.

16. Hutcheson: *An enquiry into the original of our ideas of beauty and virtue* (1725), I, i, 9.

17. Burke: *A philosophical enquiry into the original of our ideas of the sublime and the beautiful* (1757), Preface. So too Hume, *Essays* I, 23.

18. A. J. Ayer: *Language truth and logic*, ch. 6.

19. See Chapter 2, *n*. 10. Further on the point that we must know what pleases us, see Chapter 4, *n*. 9.

20. For documentation see A. Kenny: *Action emotion and will*, ch. 1.

21. Locke: *Essay*, II, ix, 8.

22. Ruskin: *Elements of drawing*, s. 5 and note.

23. If they did, how is it that Chinamen have painted English scenes from life in a Chinese style (cf. E. H. Gombrich: *Art and illusion*, fig. 63), but copying English pictures of English scenes, have produced pictures in more or less) English style (cf. *Country Life* 3 July 1969, pp. 26–7)? Since the English picture and the scene cause similar mental images in us, we would expect them to do the same for the Chinese.

24. Kant: *Critique of judgement*, s. 22, trans. J. C. Meredith, p. 86.

25. Coleridge: *Biographia literaria*, ch. 13.

26. S. Langer: *Philosophy in a new key*, ch. 4. Quoted by permission of Mrs Langer and Harvard University Press.

CHAPTER 2

1. Whistler: *Gentle art of making enemies*, pp. 127–8.

2. Whistler himself, just after the passage quoted, introduces what in Chapter 3 I call mimetic criteria: 'If the man who paints only the tree, or flower, or other surface he sees before him, were an artist, the king of artists would be the photographer. It is for the artist to do something beyond this: in portrait painting to put on canvas something more than the face the model wears for that one day; to paint the man, in short, as well as his features.'

3. Clive Bell: *Art*, ch. 1.

4. Clive Bell: *Art*, ch. 3.

5. S. Langer: *Philosophy in a new key*, ch. 8. Other passages quoted in this paragraph (by permission of Mrs Langer and Harvard University Press) come from the same chapter. Apart from her remarks about logical pictures, Mrs Langer says little which will not be found elsewhere, *e.g.* Hegel: *Philosopy of fine art*, trans. F. P. B. Osmaston, vol. III, pp. 342, 357–60.

6. See A. Harrison: 'Works of art and other cultural objects' in *Aristotelian Society Proceedings*, 1967–8; R. Woolheim: *Art and its objects*, ss. 35–7; R. Meager: 'The uniqueness of a work of art' in *Aristotelian Society Proceedings*, 1958–9; C. L. Stevenson: 'On "What is a poem" ' in *Philosophical Review*, 1957. The discussion here is chiefly of Harrison and Wollheim; on Stevenson's article see below pp. 102–3.

7. Peirce: *Collected papers* (Cambridge, Mass.), vol. 4, s. 357.

8. Usually at least. Electronic composers sometimes seem to offer exhaustive specifications, but see N. Goodman, *Languages of art*, ch. 5, s.2.

9. S. Langer: *Feeling and form*, ch. 4. Quoted by permission of Mrs Langer and Routledge and Kegan Paul Ltd.

10. See G. Ryle: *Concept of mind*, ch. 4, s. 6, and, for a fuller exposition, A. Kenny: *Action, emotion and will*, ch. 6. Both authors found suggestive the discussions in Aristotle: *Nicomachean ethics*, VII, xii and X, iii–iv.

11. A. Kenny: op cit., p. 145.

12. For impressive pioneer work on this matter, see Plato: *Philebus*, 42–7.

13. What follows is a simplified account for the convenience of readers unacquainted with the physical basis of music; such readers, however,

will find it eminently rewarding to look at Helmholtz' classic *Sensations of tone*.

14. Helmholtz: *Sensations of tone*, introduction, and cf. his final paragraph. Mrs Langer (*Philosophy in a new key*, ch. 8) says he based his 'enquiries on the assumption that music was a form of pleasurable sensation, and tried to compound the value of musical compositions out of the "pleasure elements" of their tonal constituents': this seems to be quite unjust.

15. Aquinas: *Summa theologiae*, I, xxxix, 8; see also G. Mathew: *Byzantine aesthetics*, pp. 87–90, 148–9 and *nn*.

16. Plato: *Hippias major*, 289.

17. This is argued at length by W. B. Gallie in *Philosophy and the historical understanding*, where it is a central thesis that the understanding displayed by historians is a capacity to follow a story. Although my account of following a process is intended to be more rigorous than Gallie's, much of what I say here and in Chapter 5, s. 2 was suggested by his book, and especially by his second chapter.

18. The interval of a semitone is strictly $12\sqrt{2}$ which approximates to this. Quarter-tones have been used sometimes, but not often.

19. In fact, the Greeks seem to have taken as their reference-tone a tone in the middle of an octave, corresponding to the middle string of the lyre, instead of a tone at the end. 'Why' asks the author of Aristotle: *Problems*, xix, 36, 920b 7–11 'do the other strings sound badly when the middle string is altered, but if the middle string remains and one of the others is altered, only the one altered sounds wrong? Is it not that they are all tunes, and have a certain relation, to the middle string, and the order of each is determined by that?'

20. G. Ryle: *The concept of mind*, ch. 6 s. 4. In ch. 7, s. 4, Ryle discusses following a piece of music and takes the line favoured here that listening for notes is listening to other notes in a certain way, but I do not know if he would agree that it is listening to them in such a way as to hear their pitch, loudness etc. relative to one another. He emphasises the more intellectual-sounding activities of exercising knowledge of, or trying to work out, how the music goes.

21. In saying that there is an instructive parallel between enjoying a piece of music and enjoying a hand at bridge or set at tennis, I do not mean to give any support to Schiller's view (*Letters on aesthetic education*, 27) that artistic creation and appreciation are forms of play.

22. See, for instance, E. H. Gombrich: *Art and illusion*, fig. 251.

23. See Helmholtz: *Physiological optics*, pt. II, ss. 19–20. Some of Helmholtz' conclusions have been questioned and much new material has been

assembled since he wrote, but from the aesthetician's point of view the subject has made little headway, and he is still a good introduction.

24. See R. Arnheim: *Art and visual perception*, ch. 7.

25. For an outline of gestalt theory, the student of aesthetics may prefer K. Koffka: 'Perception: an introduction to the *Gestalt-Theorie*' in *Psychological Bulletin*, 1922 to the standard *Principles of gestalt psychology* by the same author. For criticism from a philosophical standpoint, see D. W. Hamlyn: *Psychology of perception*, ch. 4.

26. So K. Mitchells: 'Aesthetic perception and aesthetic qualities' in *Aristotelian Society Proceedings*, 1966–7.

27. R. Arnheim: *Art and visual perception*, ch. 1.

28. H. Osborne: 'Artistic unity and gestalt' in *Philosophical Quarterly*, 1964.

29. So P. F. Strawson in his review in *Mind*, 1954. In fact, Osborne's theory has a more disastrous weakness: he makes the work of art proper, the thing we assess aesthetically, a structure of sensations which is an object of eighteenth-century mental awareness (*Theory of beauty*, ch. 5).

30. The notion of dynamic symmetry or commensurability in square appears in Plato: *Theaetetus*, 148.

31. These and similar phenomena are described in abundant detail by T. A. Cook: *The curves of life* (see especially ch. 5 and app. ii and ix).

32. So Cook: op. cit. and, though she seems to have other reasons as well, Mrs Langer.

33. So H. Osborne: *Theory of beauty*, especially ch. 5.

34. Some philosophers have doubted whether we ever strictly perceive change; perhaps we perceive only successive static states of affairs, like the successive frames in a cinema show, and impose the idea of change upon them. It does not seem appropriate to meet this doubt formally in a book on aesthetics, but *prima facie* it is paradoxical. We think that a thing may be changing in respect of sound for, e.g. five seconds, and that we may be aware of it by hearing for that time; why, then, should we not be aware, at any moment in that time, that it is changing and how?

CHAPTER 3

1. So K. Mitchells: 'Aesthetic perception and aesthetic qualities' in *Aristotelian Society Proceedings*, 1966–7.

2. 'Painting is a science, and should be pursued as an enquiry into the laws of nature. Why, then, may not landscape painting be considered as a branch of natural philosophy, of which pictures are but the experiments?' Constable's lecture on 16 June 1836. For Leonardo's approach, see what he says about painting in his notebooks.

3. See below, p. 80.

4. So R. Wollheim: *Art and its objects*, s. 13.

5. Against a simple equation of representation with illusion, see P. Ziff: 'Art and the "object of art" ' in *Mind*, 1951.

6. See, for instance, D. Wiggins: *Identity and spatio-temporal continuity*, especially ss. 1.6 and 4.2; J. Kovesi: *Moral notions*, ch. 1. Kovesi's chapter provides with matter for thought anyone who thinks that the passage from material to formal aspects, i.e. from our first type of account to our second, is or should be deductive.

7. cf. G. Mathew: *Byzantine aesthetics*, ch. 9, on the aesthetics of the Amorian and Macedonian period: 'The primary object of a Byzantine artist of this period was to let the formal cause become translucent through the material.'

8. This is in effect the view taken by J. L. Austin, *Sense and sensibilia*, ch. 7. I do not here wish to deny that, in Austin's idiosyncratic terminology, words like 'picture', 'dummy', 'toy', 'wear the trousers', i.e. that real is what things are until proved otherwise.

9. S. Langer: *Feeling and form*, ch. 5.

10. E. Bedford in the symposium 'Seeing paintings', *Aristotelian Society Proceedings*, suppl. vol. 1966.

11. As I think Miss R. Meager in the same symposium recognised.

12. This point seems to me worth making, because I have heard Professor G. E. L. Owen argue, in an unpublished paper, that the analogy between things in pictures and things in real life breaks down because there are criteria for reidentifying the latter but not the former.

13. pp. 15–16, 18.

14. Locke: *Essay*, II, xxi, 30.

15. See, for instance, G. Ryle: *The concept of mind*, ch. 3, s. 2; G. E. M. Anscombe: *Intention*, ss. 4, 25.

16. Descartes: *Meditations*, iii.

17. This phrase is not English; but the Greek verb for 'appearing' may be construed both with the infinitive and with the participle, and when we

have it with the participle we translate not 'it appears to be' but 'it plainly is'.

18. Berkeley: *Theory of vision vindicated*, s. 50.

19. G. J. Warnock: *Berkeley*, p. 30.

20. E. H. Gombrich: *Art and illusion*, ch. 3.

21. Berkeley: *New theory of vision*, s. 9. Berkeley does not in fact hold that seeing a man's shame by the red of his cheeks is strictly a matter of inference; but he thinks we must be conscious of the latter, and have learned to make the passage by experience.

22. e.g. Ruskin: see Chapter I, n. 22.

23. J. J. Winckelmann: *History of ancient art among the Greeks*, II, iii, 2 (trans. H. Lodge).

24. Padua, Arena chapel.

25. cf. G. Mathew: *Byzantine aesthetics*, ch. 3.

26. So Aquinas, *Summa contra gentiles*, I. 93; but the definition will have been generally acceptable.

27. Aristotle: *De partibus animalium*, I, 640^{a}31, *Metaphysics*, 1032^{b}5–14, 1070^{b}33.

28. Croce: *Aesthetic*, ch. 1.

29. Collingwood: *Principles of art* passim; see, for instance, ch. 12, s. 3.

31. G. Ryle: *The concept of mind*, ch. 8, s. 6.

32. For a similar account, see J. M. Shorter: 'Imagination' in *Mind*, 1952.

33. Collingwood: op. cit. ch. 2, s. 6.

34. Aristotle: *Poetics*, 1448^b 8–19. (The verb *manthanein* here should be translated as I have indicated and not, as it usually is, 'learn'.)

35. 'There are in fact many thousands of easel paintings which have less to communicate to the intellect than a classical Korean vase': W. H. Shewring: *Making and thinking*, p. 29. The present writer had the advantage of being taught Latin and Greek by Mr Shewring, and owes an early interest in aesthetics to *obiter dicta* of this challenging sort.

36. See above, p. 40.

37. Aquinas: *Summa theologiae*, Ia–IIae, xxvii, 1, ad 3; cf. I, v, 4, ad 1. For further source material and bibliography, see A. K. Coomaraswamy: *Why exhibit works of art*, ch. 2; *Figures of speech or figures of thought*, ch. 2.

38. As was observed by J. Maritain: *Art and scholasticism*, n. 55.

39. pp. 20–1.

40. It would be out of place to attempt a detailed justification of this interpretation here. The reader may look especially at *Critique of judgement*, introduction, ss. v–viii, and 'Deduction of pure aesthetic judgements', ss. 35–8.

41. For a recent discussion of formalism in Kant's aesthetics see R. L. Zimmermann: 'Kant: the aesthetic judgement' in *Journal of aesthetics and art criticism*, 1962–3 (reprinted in R. P. Wolff, Ed.: *Kant, a collection of critical essays*.

42. Eric Gill: *Beauty looks after herself*, p. 231.

43. Eric Gill: *Art*, ch. 1.

44. Plato: *Republic*, X, 597.

45. Plato: *Cratylus*, 389.

46. Quoted by W. H. Shewring: *Making and thinking*, p. 23.

47. A. K. Coomaraswamy: see, for instance, the essays on 'Hindu view of art' in *The dance of Siva*.

48. Plotinus: *Enneads*, III, viii, 4.

49. Plotinus: *Enneads*, III, viii passim (on contemplation generally and trees, earth etc.); V, i, 3 and 7; ix, 5 (on the Soul, Mind, Ideas etc.)

50. i.e. it is wrong to analyse 'It represents a bed' as 'There is a bed it represents', and similarly wrong to analyse 'It is (constitutes) a bed' as 'There is a bed it is (constitutes)'.

51. Hegel: see *Philosophy of fine art*, introduction, ch. 5.

52. For some critical remarks about essentialism in aesthetics, see W. B. Gallie: 'The function of philosophical aesthetics' in *Mind*, 1948.

53. A. K. Coomaraswamy: *The dance of Siva*, pp. 36–7, cf. 39–45.

54. Eric Gill: *Beauty looks after herself*, p. 266.

55. ibid. p. 216. It is remarkable that although Gill in general sets out to attack Bell's theory of art, he shares with Bell the belief that the notion of ultimate reality has a star part to play in aesthetics.

CHAPTER 4

1. Wordsworth: Preface to *Lyrical Ballads* (2nd ed.). This is generally considered an early statement of the expressionist view, but Mrs Langer is able to quote C. P. E. Bach as evidence that eighteenth-century

musicians conceived themselves as conveying their own emotions to the audience: *Philosophy in a new key*, ch. 8.

2. Collingwood: *Principles of art*. The doctrines I attribute to him will be found in chs. 8, s. 2 (sensa and their emotional charges), 11 (a fairly complete statement of the theory), 12, s. 3 (good and bad art), and 13, s. 3 (philosophy). For other philosophical developments of the expressionist theory see Croce: *Aesthetic*, and E. F. Carritt: *Theory of beauty*. See also, for a critical discussion, J. Hospers: 'The Croce–Collingwood theory of art' in *Philosophy*, 1956.

3. cf. G. Pitcher: 'Emotions' in *Mind*, 1965; Pitcher uses the expressions 'occurrent' and 'dispositional emotions'.

4. Aristotle claims that moral dispositions or virtues can be defined as dispositions to feel the right things at the right times towards the right objects (the ability to see what is right here being *phronesis* or prudence): *Nicomachaen ethics*, II, vi, 1106^{b}16–1107^{a}2.

5. A. Kenny: *Action, emotion and will*, ch. 3, p. 71. Kenny follows Miss Anscombe: *Intention*, s. 10, who follows Wittgenstein: *Philosophical investigations*, I, s. 476. The distinction between causes and objects drawn by Hume (*Treatise*, II, i, 2) is different.

6. Discussed by J. C. Gosling: 'Mental causes and fear' in *Mind*, 1962.

7. So R. Wollheim: 'Thought and passion' in *Aristotelian Society Proceedings*, 1967–8.

8. See A. Kenny: op. cit., ch. 9, p. 189.

9. It is a pity that Kenny does not use these distinctions in his analysis of pleasure. He thinks that 'A schoolboy at a dormitory feast imagines he is enjoying eating cold bacon and burnt potatoes when he is really enjoying the illicitness of his escapade' (op. cit., p. 131). The suggestion is the odd one that we must know the material object of our enjoyment, but need not know the formal. I prefer the diagnosis of the author of the example (J. C. Gosling: *Phronesis*, 1959, p. 49) that the illicitness of what the schoolboy is doing 'enables him to overlook the deficiencies of the cuisine', i.e. is not the object but rather the cause of the pleasure. The schoolboy is indeed enjoying eating bacon and potatoes, but the school authorities disposed him to enjoy this activity in these circumstances by their prohibitions.

10. Aristotle: *Rhetoric*, II, 1378^{a}31–3, 1382^{a}21–2.

11. This is emphasised by M. Perkins: 'Emotion and feeling' in *Philosophical Review*, 1966.

12. *Qui enim imaginatur mulierem, quam amat, alteri sese prostituere, non solum ex eo, quod ipsius appetitus coercetur, contristabitur; sed etiam,*

quia rei amatae imaginem pudendis, et excrementis alterius jungere cogitur, eandem aversatur. In general Spinoza's account of emotion is similar to that recommended here. Emotions are defined by their objects, and the connection between how we think of things and how we act is logical.

13. This is how Spinoza seems to conceive the 'passive' emotions which enslave a man: see *Ethics*, III, especially the definitions at the end.

14. So J. C. Gosling: 'Emotion and object' in *Philosophical Review*, 1965.

15. S. Langer: *Philosophy in a new key*, ch. 4. Compare Collingwood on 'this quite peculiar anger', op. cit., ch. 6, s. 3.

16. Proust: *Le temps retrouvé*, ch. 3.

17. Proust: *Du côté de chez Swann*, I, 2.

18. e.g. F. R. Leavis: *The great tradition*, ch. 1. This approach is discussed at some length from a philosophical angle by J. Casey: *The language of criticism*, chs. 8 and 9.

19. This is how it is usually treated today, e.g. by M. Clark: 'Humour and incongruity' in *Philosophy* 1970.

20. Kant: *Critique of judgement*, s. 54.

21. Plato: *Philebus*, 48–50.

22. E. F. Carritt: *Theory of beauty*, app. A.

23 cf. O. K. Bouwsma: 'The expression theory of art' in M. Black (Ed.): *Philosophical Analysis*.

24. The example of Aristotle, who drew attention to this way of using words in *Metaphysics*, 1003^{a}33–^{b}1 and elsewhere.

25. B. Berenson: *Italian painters of the renaissance*, II, ii.

CHAPTER 5

1. Professor J. Margolis suggests that *reading* a work of literature stands to the work read as a performance to the music performed: 'The logic of aesthetic judgement' in *Philsophical Quarterly*, 1959. This seems a little far-fetched.

2. C. L. Stevenson 'On "What is a poem" ' in *Philosophical Review*, 1957.

3. Shakespeare: *The Tempest*, I, ii.

4. Homer: *Odyssey*, V, 239.

5. In *Mind*, 1950.

6. J. L. Austin: *How to do things with words*, lectures 8 ff.

7. cf. E. J. Lemmon: 'Sentences, statements and propositions' in B. Williams and A. Montefiore Eds.: *British analytical philosophy*. What Lemmon calls propositions I call assertions and denials.

8. Shakespeare: *Sonnet* 106.

9. The fullest discussion is perhaps C. L. Stevenson: *Ethics and Language*, ch. 3. See also Stevenson's *Facts and values*, ch. 2, s. 3: P. H. Nowell-Smith: *Ethics*, ch. 7, s. 1; R. M. Hare: *Language of morals*, ch. 7.

10. Homer: *Iliad*, VI, 146–9.

11. J. Benson: 'Emotion and expression' in *Philosophical Review*, 1967.

12. W. K. Wimsatt and Monroe T. Beardsley: 'The intentional fallacy' reprinted (from W. K. Wimsatt: *The verbal icon*) with select bibliography in J. Margolis (Ed.): *Philosophy looks at the arts*.

13. So A. Savile: 'The place of intention in the concept of art' in *Aristotelian Society Proceedings*, 1968–9.

14. So F. Cioffi: 'Intention and interpretation in criticism' in *Aristotelian Society Proceedings*, 1963–4.

15. Catullus 51; Sappho fr. 31. I am grateful to Mr C. J. Fordyce for the Gladstone version.

16. Shakespeare: *Sonnet* 73. (This example is also discussed by Cioffi: see n. 14 above.)

17. Nine, if he followed the precept of *Ars Poetica*, 388 (and over some of the Odes he apparently did).

18. Collingwood: *Principles of art*, ch. 6, s. 7. Collingwood is in fact speaking of actors, but his theory requires him to say the same of poets.

19. cf. Spinoza: *Ethics*, III, 48. Spinoza, like Collingwood, stresses the importance of becoming conscious of our emotions, but he has a very different idea of how we do this.

20. Mrs Langer falls into the same mistake as Collingwood. She says that a ballerina who wants to dance a gay dance ought to imagine the feelings she would have if she were on holiday in California (sic); it would be better, surely, for her to imagine California.

21.   *Te flagrantis atrox hora Caniculae*
                  nescit tangere, tu frigus amabile
                        fessis vomere tauris
                            praebes et pecori vago. (Odes, III, 13, 9–12)

Much of Horace's time was probably spent in thinking of the sound and order of his words, and this is even less a matter of being moved to a burst of poetry by a total sensory and emotional experience.

22. Shakespeare: *Sonnet* 66.

23. Hume: *Treatise*, I, iii, 7.

24. Plato: *Cratylus*, 430–1. Plato reached a more incisive account of speech in the *Sophist* (see especially *Sophist*, 261–2).

25. So R. M. Hare: *Language of morals*, ch. 2.

26. Russell: 'On denoting' in *Mind*, 1905; cf. his 'Knowledge by acquaintance and knowledge by description' in *Aristotelian Society Proceedings*, 1910–11. Russell has stated firmly (*Mind*, 1957) that his analysis was not intended to illuminate anything except the logical form of propositions, but its relevance to other matters has often been discussed.

27. G. Ryle: 'Imaginary objects' in *Aristotelian Society Proceedings*, suppl. vol. 1933.

28. G. Ryle: *The concept of mind*, chs. 6, s. 4, 8, s. 3. (The suggestion is made only in passing.)

29. Thucydides, III, 42–9.

30. For an example, unfortunate because the idea he is trying to express is a good one, see Locke: Essay II, xxvii, 4, the last sentence. Contrast the lucidity of Hume's most notorious arguments, e.g. *Treatise* III, i, 1, Ed. Selby-Bigge, pp. 267–9.

31. See Chapter 2, n. 17.

32. Aristotle: *Poetics*, 1450ª38–9. For a philosophical discussion of Aristotle's account of tragedy, see the symposium 'Tragedy' in *Aristotelian Society Proceedings*, suppl. vol. 1960.

INDEX